S0-AWN-478

RECEIVED

MAY 0 9 2022

GREEN LAKE BRANCH

NO LONGER PROPERTY
SEATTLE PUBLIC LIBRARY

Not Dead Yet

Not Dead Yet

Rebooting Your Life after 50

Barbara Ballinger and Margaret Crane

ROWMAN & LITTLEFIELD
Lanham • Boulder • New York • London

Published by Rowman & Littlefield
A wholly owned subsidiary of The Rowman & Littlefield Publishing Group, Inc.
4501 Forbes Boulevard, Suite 200, Lanham, Maryland 20706
www.rowman.com

6 Tinworth Street, London SE11 5AL, United Kingdom

Copyright © 2021 by The Rowman & Littlefield Publishing Group, Inc.

All rights reserved. No part of this book may be reproduced in any form or by
any electronic or mechanical means, including information storage and retrieval
systems, without written permission from the publisher, except by a reviewer who
may quote passages in a review.

British Library Cataloguing in Publication Information Available

Library of Congress Cataloging-in-Publication Data

Names: Ballinger, Barbara (Barbara B.), author. | Crane, Margaret, author.
Title: Not dead yet : rebooting your life after 50 / Barbara Ballinger and
    Margaret Crane.
Description: Lanham : Rowman & Littlefield, [2021] | Includes bibliographical
    references and index.
Identifiers: LCCN 2020057514 (print) | LCCN 2020057515 (ebook) | ISBN
    9781538148495 (cloth) | ISBN 9781538148501 (ebook)
Subjects: LCSH: Older people—Social conditions. | Aging—Social aspects.
Classification: LCC HQ1061 .B34 2021 (print) | LCC HQ1061 (ebook) | DDC
    305.26—dc23
LC record available at https://lccn.loc.gov/2020057514
LC ebook record available at https://lccn.loc.gov/2020057515

For Nolan E. Crane and Estelle C. Ballinger
You will always be in our hearts.

Contents

Acknowledgments

As life throws us curveballs when least expected, it's up to us to hit them out of the park.

During the last few years, we have become better prepared to catch what comes our way whether it impacted our lives, our family and friends, or the planet, as the coronavirus pandemic of 2020 did. Isolated, we each worked alone on this book during that horrific period, fortunate to have the technology to send ideas and chapters back and forth and talk daily.

There are so many we wish to thank for help in navigating our journeys of the last few years. We start with our literary agent, Kelli Christiansen of Bibliobibuli. She has listened and laughed as we talked, sometimes *ad nauseum*, about how we had changed since we worked with her on our last book. She always shared her honest input, tweaked or even rewrote our copy, and was at the head of the line cheerleading for us when we finished a chapter or the manuscript. We are now a seasoned three-person team.

We thank our editor Suzanne Staszak-Silva at our publisher, Rowman & Littlefield, and her colleagues Melissa McClellan and Barbara Jarrett. We couldn't have done it without your comments, suggestions, patience, and compliments to keep us going. We also thank our many friends, work colleagues, tech gurus, acquaintances, and experts from so many different professions. You shared your stories and advice to provide us with greater depth and lessons that anyone alone and older might learn from. You read what we wrote to check quotes and attribution. Accuracy has always been very important to us. There are too many to list each of you, but we wish to thank all.

We thank friends who read early versions sometimes repeatedly or looked at cover and website designs. To Fixup, Lucy Leibowitz, Marilyn Liss, Carol Lundgren, Tracy Maurice, Susan Van Raalte, Judy Rubin, and Sue White, we appreciate your time and candor.

We thank our families for letting us tell our stories honestly and authentically. We believe we have remembered personal stories, places, and dates well, and if we didn't quite capture every nuance perfectly, forgive us. After all, we are now officially old, as the pandemic of 2020 and our grown children informed us repeatedly. Thank you also for putting up with us when we were going through some of our greatest challenges, repeated ourselves, rambled, and cried. You calmed us down, listened, let us be abrupt at times, laughed along with us, and applauded us when we finished writing this book.

Of course, we continue to think of Nolan. You were with us every step of the way—when we wrote about parenting, barbecuing, gardening, consuming wine, entertaining, music, being an enthusiastic partner and friend, enduring pain, and losing out on life too early. How much you would have marveled at how well Margaret has done finding her way alone, though she isn't alone, as this book attests. We know you would have handled the old-age stage and changes gracefully.

We also think of Estelle, and how well she navigated old age. Sadly, she died as we were finishing the manuscript. Barbara wanted to read it to her for her input. We both consider her passing to be a huge loss.

If we have one final lesson to share that's been echoed by many, it's this: Grab on to happiness whenever you can. Buy the leopard shoes you crave. Take the trip you've dreamed about. Spend a year in Paris. Drink the wine (before it becomes vinegar). Gobble up the expensive chocolate before it melts. Make the move. Hug the friends and family. Shed the toxic people who stop you from relishing joyful moments. Tell those you care about how much you love them, say it often, and say it out loud now. And most important, live in the present and be grateful for every single day.

Barbara Ballinger and Margaret Crane
November 2020

Authors' Note

When we wrote our last book, *Suddenly Single After 50: The Girl-friends' Guide to Navigating Loss, Restoring Hope, and Rebuilding Your Life*, we thought we were well positioned to effortlessly navigate life as single women.

How cocky and naïve we were.

After almost five years, and now in our 70s, we slowly realized that the aging process had caught up with us—and many of our friends, family members, work colleagues, and people we regularly encountered.

The best prescription to find joy in these older years, we decided, was to live life more fully in the moment. Less looking back; what's past is past. As dogged researchers, we put a laser focus on how we could best do that, which meant analyzing how we spend our time.

We noted both what we needed to do to improve our own happiness quotients rather than anybody else's and what we were supposed to do now as official members of the older cohort. The COVID-19 pandemic of 2020 (and our kids) hammered home the message that we were part of this demographic.

This stage has become one of the most difficult, challenging passages in our lives. Andy Rooney, the late American radio and television writer, said, "Life is like a roll of toilet paper. The closer you get to the end, the faster it goes." As we near the finish line, we decided it was up to us—and only us—to decide how we should live out our lives.

Gradually, we started feeling stronger, more empowered, happier, and more in control, despite the rough patches that continue to occur.

We've learned the hard way that what happens today can change in a flash. Change is rarely easy regardless of age, finances, and status. We know, too, that we have been privileged, made more obvious when the COVID-19 pandemic of 2020 hit. We worried about our health and our loved ones as we isolated ourselves and kept our distances in our safe homes. As we read about the disproportionate numbers of underserved people becoming infected and dying, it raised our level of consciousness about how lucky we are and what each of us could do to help those less fortunate.

This book is about our older-age journeys, decisions, failures, losses, and successes, which we continue to discuss and agonize about with each other. We have come up with six major concerns as we age and try to live joyfully: where we will live next if we don't stay put, how we will maintain a circle of friends and family, if we will have enough money to live comfortably, how we will spend our time and feel useful, and how we will cope with physical and emotional challenges that arise. We asked other women of our vintage—and men (many of whom asked to have only their first names or a pseudonym used to preserve anonymity) how they balance these realities. Their stories are interspersed among ours throughout the book.

We remind ourselves—and others—that we can best lessen the angst and disappointments of aging if we focus on the people we are most thankful for. In our cases that includes five children, two grandchildren, one partner, siblings, cousins, and friends. These relationships count so much because they confirm that we are never alone. We both also remain open to the notion that we will continue to evolve since we are committed to following our core belief: We're Not Dead Yet.

—Barbara Ballinger and Margaret Crane, November 2020

Foreword

It is a truth universally acknowledged that a single man of three score and ten (70-plus years old) is in search of a nurse or a purse.

A truth less often acknowledged is that a woman of three score and ten is not looking for a man who has hair in his ears and will, in no more than a few years, trade Viagra for Depends.

And it is a truth, even less acknowledged, that a man of three score and ten years who has his hair, some money, meaningful work, and reasonable health will have an easier time climbing Everest in sneakers than finding a suitable woman.

That is my story. The end of my marriage coincided with the beginning of my third score and tenth year. I can hunt and gather, but I prefer domesticity, and I set off to find my next victim.

Instinct directed me to M. Like me, she worked in media. We traveled in the same social circles. She was sane and solvent. Our stars seemed to align. I confessed: "I'm terrified to sleep with you." She said the same. "Yes," I said, "but I haven't felt that since I was 19." She was still mourning her partner of 30 years, dead for four. We never went to bed.

S. also worked in media. She also traveled in my social circle. We went to bed, early and often. Alas, she forgot to tell me she had borderline personality disorder, so I was blindsided when she broke up with me at dinner. I moved on to dating sites. I avoided women who were looking for their "last first date," who liked "spicy red wine" at "new restaurants," and believed "cuddle" was foreplay for sex, but I still encountered sad or angry women who were instantly toting up my imperfections.

Could I convert female friends to lovers? Almost without exception, they said, "That shop is closed."

In a parallel universe, I would have happily tumbled for Barbara Ballinger or Margaret Crane. They have been battered—one is a widow, one is divorced—but they're not broken. On the contrary: Their souls are powered by the notion that there must be a bright light to cast such dark shadows.

Just as important, they're realists. They know a seasoned prince isn't looking for a princess. You want a vibrant life and maybe even a partner? Fix yourself first.

They ask all the right questions:

- Your home. Are you doubling down on your current home because it feels safe, even if you find your community thinning out?
- Your community of friends: if it's shrinking, how can you grow it?
- Your money. Even Jackie Kennedy worried that an overlong old age would condemn her to poverty. You may want to adjust your situation sooner rather than later.
- Time management. Picasso said, "We become young at 60, and then it's too late." He lied—he painted to the end. Your life is a race, but not to death. If you have work or hobbies you care about, you too can run through the tape.
- Your mental and physical health. Decline is inevitable. How will you cope?

Ballinger and Crane draw on their own experience, but this is not one of those braggy self-help books in which the only people to benefit are the authors and their publisher. They've cast a wide net. They've talked to women who aren't like them. And then they wrote a book that's actually helpful—even, dare I say it, to men.

Jesse Kornbluth, HeadButler.com, is a playwright, who wrote *The Color of Light*, about Henri Matisse.

Chapter One

Learning to Live in the Moment

The Yiddish proverb, "We Plan, God Laughs," had new meaning for each of us when we both lost our spouses and suddenly were on our own after long-term marriages.

We never imagined ourselves as singles. We believed we would always be part of a couple who would live happily ever after. That implied forever. How presumptuous we discovered we were when the bottom dropped out of each of our lives.

We learned so much as we struggled with our losses. Life as a single meant we had to master being alone. Many do and are quite happy. Some never marry out of choice. That was not the path either of us chose.

We each liked married life. We imagined retiring and growing old as a couple. When life didn't work out that way, we might have remained stuck. But we each found after a few months (Barbara) or two years (Margaret) that remaining paralyzed didn't work. We had grown children and aging parents who depended on us. We had close friends who pushed us out of our nests of heartbreaking solitude.

We both had strong gut feelings that tugged at us to tap into our resiliency and reengage. We once were funny and loved to laugh. Where had our humor gone? Maybe down the toilet? We once had good instincts about what to do, when, and with whom. It was time to become more self-aware and motivated, put one foot in front of the other—that's what feet are for, right? Life wasn't to be wasted or taken for granted.

So, when our internal time clocks urged us to rediscover our strength, we gathered our forces—friends, family, and professionals, who had dealt with others in similar straits. We learned we weren't the only ones to face such heartache.

We listened to everyone's advice since we adhere to the philosophy that we need a village for a variety of ideas before we reach a decision. Once we had a plan, life began to slowly kick in again as we paid bills, got back to work, earned money, exercised, traveled, cooked, found our funny bones, and cobbled together a social life, but this time as singles. And we did all without overeating, drinking, or taking drugs.

Was it smooth going as we charted our new paths? Hell no. We made huge mistakes along the way with friends, romantic relationships, work, family, and outside interests. Barbara regretted dating too quickly and too much. She felt she wasted time looking for Mr. Right when she found so many Mr. Wrongs. Margaret dated an old high school boyfriend, but the relationship slowly died after more than three years.

Then, gradually, we surprised ourselves. We recognized that we loved being on our own now that our lives had changed. Living alone became empowering and even joyous once we got in touch with our new, inner selves. Being alone had moments of levity, too. We could do outrageous things when nobody watched. We screamed at the TV when we didn't like the politics we heard, disco danced to Donna Summer's music while vacuuming, threw clothing on the floor and left it for days just because we could, or walked around buck naked and didn't hear such comments as: "Hum, you need to shed a few," unless we talked to ourselves. And we did that plenty, too, which most who live alone tend to do.

We came through our upheaval and made big adjustments. Were we finished and fine for now and forever? We thought so at the time. As others agonized about the big 7-0 number looming, we thumbed our noses, and thought, "Seventy is just a number, a piece of cake. We've been through so much more that this pales by comparison." Sadly, we forgot that we might feel young inside, but life isn't that simple. Or, aging isn't.

Surprise! Turning 70 for us—and others—was the start of a new colossal uphill chapter of losses and challenges related to us, family, and friends. (For others it can be the big 50 or 60.) If our bodies were cars, we joked, we'd trade them in for newer models as our parts began creaking and breaking down. For some of us our memories began to fade. Recalling certain words and events took longer, "Oh, the word is on the tip of my tongue." Aches and pains showed up unbidden. Habits we once considered okay began to creep up on us and bring new consequences, whether from eating too much sugar, being overly sedentary, repeating ourselves, or asking too often, "Huh, what did you say?" We each spent entire meals with friends shaking our heads up and down to appear like we heard what others were saying. We were too ashamed to admit that we had heard few words. Maybe it was time for hearing aids, a wretched visible sign that, *oy, we are old.* At the same time, we consumed more pills, tried to remember which ones we took when, and put up Post-it® notes around our homes as reminders, had more procedures and surgeries, and made more appointments with physical therapists and doctors, including psychotherapists for emotional challenges.

Then one day when writing our weekly blog, lifelessonsat50plus. com, we had a bombshell moment when one of us said to the other, "You know what? We've made some great strides, even though our lives are dramatically different from our former ones. However, we've hit a new stage of old age that has crept up on us. There's so much we must do with the time we have left."

Margaret began to talk of downsizing and moving. Barbara questioned her latest home, which was supposed to be her forever place, saying, "I love it, but it seems too large and expensive now." We drove each other insane debating. And then we laughed and realized, thank goodness, we have choices and still each other to drive insane.

Life is too short to complain. It was up to us to figure it out sooner rather than later, get up, get out, enjoy life, and tidy up, as joy expert Marie Kondo instructed us to do with our homes. That was the beginning. There was decluttering of familial and friend relationships, our bodies, and our minds. Just as a messy desk can be a deterrent to doing work, so is a cluttered and worried brain an obstacle to focusing on what's important.

It became time to sign legal documents, have necessary discussions, and tend to meaningful relationships while we could. We each started to make changes: eat cleaner; jump-start a more age-appropriate fitness regimen; find our inner calm; set better boundaries with friends, adult children, and aging parents; and look into where we might live if we couldn't stay in our homes, even if someday we'd have to move again.

But we also advised ourselves that moving and adjusting to new places, people, and routines requires great energy and becomes harder after 70. The good news is that we each still have a lot of living to do. By eliminating what and who is less important, we have time for new challenges. We might jump out of that plane, find a new career or hobby, go on a date and have sex—or not—learn a language, make a difference by giving our time and money to a worthy volunteer cause. Who knows? There are so many charms still to add to the bracelet of our lives.

We decided our new mantra would be to get going now while we can as we and so many women and men we talked to have started to do. Although we love to plan, we realize the importance of consciously living in the moment.

Chapter Two

We're How Old Now?

Women Who Are Age-Defiers

As we look back on our lives, they have been rich and full of love and rewards, even in hard times. On our birthdays each decade, family and friends hosted lovely parties for us. They congratulated us and said with straight faces that we looked 50 years old at 60 and 60 years old at 70. It was true at most times because we took better care of ourselves than most of our parents and grandparents did.

Yet, we are old. It hurts to say this, but it's true. Almost every time we now have a medical problem, we hear the advice prefaced with: "At your age. . . ." The heck with that kind of thinking. We are trying to live our lives to be healthy, happy age-defiers.

We both are crusaders for singing the praises of the mind-body-spirit connection. We care about how we look, get our hair colored and cut well, use special moisturizers and makeup, buy clothes that flatter our changing figures, get regular medical checkups, avoid too much screen time, try to sleep enough, and maintain connections with people to forestall loneliness.

However, aging can be tough. Our bodies have changed. We have the scars, stretch marks, cellulite, and sagging boobs to prove it. When younger, our bodies moved effortlessly and would do what we asked them to do. Now they ache at times when we move, so we adjust. There are activities we cannot—or should not—do, such as ice skating for fear of falling and breaking aging bones. We have toned down the running, and bicycling, and go slower. We swim fewer laps, and we opted out of jumping jacks and other high-impact aerobic exercises for fear of stress fractures. We huff and puff when we climb a long run of stairs or hills. In this new phase of our lives, we favor safe lower-key, balance- and core-enhancing power walking, Pilates, and yoga. When we sneeze or laugh too hard, we fear the dreaded urine leakage that comes with age known as weakened pelvic floor muscles.

Fortunately, as old parts falter, there are new treatments and replacements. Overall, we feel healthy, as do many of our friends and family members, though most of us are on more medications and vitamin supplements (natural, of course). Entire conversations with friends revolve around who takes which pills, what doses, how often, how we swallow large ones, side effects from some, and whether most meds help. We laugh about the fact that we've now hit this stage of ills and pills. How did this happen?

Due to the health challenges we face in these advanced years, we see doctors more often and put those we frequent on speed dial. To be ahead of the game, we updated our wills, living wills, health proxies, power of attorney, and purchased long-term care insurance if our financial experts advised doing so. (See chapter 7 for details.)

We accept that we're aging. And let us stress, we are not looking to return to the heady days of youth. We know that's not possible, despite what some advertisements might suggest. However, there are so many ways to find appropriate experiences and trappings even after the age of 60, 70, and beyond.

You might be able to spend money and time in a beauty salon changing the color of your hair and adding highlights, or you can color it yourself with good drugstore products. You can get lured into wearing short skirts, which can be an eyesore at a certain age unless you still have fabulous legs without varicose veins. You can even hobble on high heels if you want, like House Speaker Nancy Pelosi—but, ouch, how painful. You can hand a good chunk of your retirement money over to a plastic surgeon for tucks around the eyes, chin, neck, or all, if it's in your budget. Some of us consider or begin to go more regularly for Botox injections, liposuction, and other fillers.

We stare at emerging wrinkles and age spots and wonder who that face is in the mirror, and, yikes, it's our own. Then, we go buy some magic face cream touted to erase the wrinkles. Our hair is thinning. Some of us are dotted with liver spots, have flabby arms, and try to hide bulging waistlines by wearing loose untucked shirts. Ironically, those wrinkles, liver spots, and other signs of aging often help us get discounts at some restaurants, movie theaters, concerts, and retail stores. There's also major cosmetic surgery, which the two of us have avoided for financial and health reasons. We're not against it for others. However, the outcomes cannot be fully guaranteed, even with top physicians. A friend of Barbara's went to one of her city's best cosmetic surgeons for a neck lift and continues to have pain.

Although Barbara loathes her neck, as much as writer Nora Ephron did and made famous in her book, *I Feel Bad about My Neck: And Other Thoughts on Being a Woman,* she has learned to live with it. As much as we may dislike the physical changes happening as we age, there are noninvasive treatments to counteract them. To feel and look better, Barbara loves an occasional, relatively inexpensive facial.

Despite the changes in our looks and our shorter heights due to "age shrinkage," there are advantages to having lived this long. We've each been lucky to have experienced many happy times—first homes, births of children and grandchildren, school graduations, weddings, job promotions. But these haven't precluded tragic events as well: the death of loved ones, including four parents; Margaret's husband, Nolan; and numerous relatives and good friends. They've died from cancer, heart disease, dementia, suicide, and old age. We've shown compassion, sympathy, and empathy as others battle those and other challenges, including loneliness, anxiety, and depression.

It's also a time of uncertainty—most of life is—about what might happen. What if we fall and break a leg or a hip, shoulder, or wrist? How will that affect our lifestyle, work, and finances? Barbara had surgery almost five years ago for two broken bones and a fractured wrist of her dominant right hand after a fall on her icy driveway. She had to adjust when typing with her left hand for a full month, and then she had to adjust through the pain again when going back to using her injured right hand as part of the therapy. She worries each winter about falling, so she walks slowly in boots with cleats through snow and ice. She jokes that she was lucky it happened after she turned 65 and was on Medicare since the bills were steep. Thankfully, her medical expenses were covered.

We know each of us has become hypervigilant at times about our health as we age, imagining a cough as the precursor of a viral infection, some urine discomfort to be a harbinger of a serious bladder infection or the beginning of kidney cancer, a lapse in memory to be the first sign of dementia.

Maybe that's our way not to tempt the fates with our overall good health—so far. However, what if we didn't have good medical care? Not everyone does. Who will care for those among us who are single for whatever reason or who might not have family and children to care for us as we age? What if our children or nieces and nephews or younger friends do not live nearby? What about those who don't have funds to pay for caregivers or nursing care but cannot live independently? Who wants to live in an assisted living facility or nursing home after so many died in such places during the COVID-19 pandemic of 2020?

What can we do instead? Should we plan now, while we're healthy, to downsize if our homes are too large and have too many stairs, area rugs, slippery bathroom floors, bathtubs we can't climb over, showers without zero thresholds, and high-up cabinet storage? Should we install grab bars or at least specify blocks in our walls that make it cheaper and easier to install the bars later? How about wall-to-wall carpeting instead of chic but slippery tile or hardwood floors?

A lot of questions and "what ifs" come with aging. We know we can adapt; we've done it before. But just about everything can be so much harder when we get older, especially if we're not as mobile or mentally sharp.

Because we've faced loss and survived, we've become more resilient when challenges come our way. However, many new ones can't always be fixed. We try to complain less often about the mundane stuff that echoes our own parents' laments, whether it's grown kids not calling or visiting us enough; gaining a few pounds; trying to read miniscule fine print without a magnifying glass, reading glasses, or enlarging the font; or no longer having the same energy level we once did. We figure it's useless to waste time brooding over a slight from a stranger or lose sleep over events that may or may not occur in the distant future. This is the time to be positive and focus on what gives us pleasure.

We also try to erase from our hard drives the angst, worry, and, if possible, negative thoughts. And we remind ourselves—hey, aging person, the world is still yours to enjoy! This is particularly true as some of us retire and others scale back work. Many of us still choose to work and find great pleasure from it. Others need to work for the extra income, even after taking Social Security. In both situations, work can keep aging brains active, sustain souls, and help pay the bills we keep accumulating. Bills don't stop just because we're old.

Overall, many of us have never had this luxury of so much unscheduled time: fewer commitments, unless self-imposed, and fewer demands—unless we seek them out. We fancy our days as languid stretches of time. Many of our friends tell us that, in the mornings, they snuggle back under their warm covers and get up whenever they please. We might take a walk, stop to visit friends face-to-face rather than connect online. (During the COVID-19 pandemic of 2020 we wore our masks and practiced social distancing, of course.) When together in person or via technology, we vent about politics, the weather, and, yes, aging.

During these twilight years, we no longer feel we need to rush through life. With so many choices of things to do, we try not to get overwhelmed or feel new pressures. If we don't want to read the book recommended by our book club, the hell with it. This isn't school with grades. We contend, if we try to do just one healthy thing a day, why not do it? Maybe we'll sit outside on a bench and enjoy the so-called fresh air. It's about immersing your senses in the natural world to disconnect from stress and improve well-being, which the Japanese call forest bathing.

We've mastered many of these lessons as we watched up close the really old grow older and see how they handled it—in good and bad ways. Margaret's mother lived to age 92, and in her last 10 years, she was loath to venture out and then she couldn't do so. After several falls and emergency runs to the hospital, she was afraid to move. She'd spend her days in bed watching TV and sleeping. Watching her mother give up on life too soon, Margaret thought, "What a waste."

Mild dementia set in for her mother. By the time she hit 90 years old, she was immobile and so afraid to leave the security of her bedroom that the depression meds she finally went on did little good beyond elevating her mood a bit. She was more pleasant to be around, but her four children and six grandchildren found her situation tragic. To live a life with little joy and too many health challenges seems not enough to live for. Margaret's philosophy became: Grab what time is left and make good use of it in whatever way possible.

Barbara's mother hit the century mark in fall 2019. Up until her 99th birthday, she was in remarkable shape, able to walk with the help of a cane or walker; read large-print books despite macular degeneration; and enjoy a good appetite, with sweets a much-favored food because of her changing taste buds. Not the healthiest option, but at that age, who cares? (Barbara did.) Her memory remained intact, and she had a zest for living—enjoying visits from family and a few remaining friends and weekly services at her temple. She welcomed some additional help from Barbara and later paid certified health-care aides. Her mother took old age in stride, telling others "We live too long." Barbara and Margaret, who visited Barbara's mother, noted her slow decline, and began thinking more about their own futures.

We've also taken notice of other much older relatives, friends, and people who inspire us and who are still active and basically healthy. They show us how to live well:

• "Sally," 82, has shown us not to let small things get us down, including heartaches with our own family members. Despite losing her mother when she was aged five and being raised by her aunt and uncle because her father's new wife preferred not to have the baggage of someone else's young daughter, she learned early about the absence of permanence. But she grew up in a loving home with a cousin-turned-brother and learned from aunts and uncles about the importance of family. "They showed by example and never missed holidays, birthdays, talking to each other, and visiting their mother, who owned a store. It was an amazing family to be part of," she says. She also married well at age 19, and she and her spouse have shared more than 60 years together. She takes advantage of every minute with her go-go style and strong sense of spirituality and values. She worries about health challenges but looks them squarely in the eye with the attitude that she can find the best expert available to help when she needs it. She exercises daily and eats well, and she has created lovely homes, traveled well, and made friends easily. She jokes that she can talk to anyone because she involves herself in life and is always curious. But she knows if all disappears, the trappings aren't important. "I'm a survivor," Sally says. "I wake up every day and tell myself it's going to be a good day, especially since I woke up! Attitude is so important. Age is only a number." Best of all, she says, might be that her four grandkids think she is cool.

- Ruth, 96, has been a friend of Barbara's family since the early 1950s. She has a razor-sharp mind and other age-defying characteristics. Twenty-one years into a wonderful marriage, she lost her first husband when she was 43 and he 46, with three sons still at home or in college. She remarried after a blind date and helped raise her second husband's three children, masterfully blending their families. With husband no. 2, she had 30 years of happiness, which included involvement in his fast-paced, impressive television journalism career. After he died following a series of strokes, she continued his work for another 17 years. During that time, she became romantically involved with a long-time friend (a retired doctor), and they remained a loving, tight couple until he died. She continues her zest for life with her blended brood of six, five daughters-in-law, 10 grandchildren, and two great-grandchildren. She has given up driving due to poor vision but still is on the go from her large three-story home near Manhattan, heading off to her weekend home in the country, concerts, theater, lectures, and regular dinners out with friends and family. And she looks terrific and stylish. Her secrets? A loving, attentive, supportive family network—and shredded wheat for breakfast every morning.

- Sonia Warshawski, 95, the mother of one of Margaret's good friends who lives in Kansas City, Kansas, is a Holocaust survivor whose life has never been richer. She is healthy, lives independently in the home she's owned for 50 years, and requires no walking aids. Recently, Sonia's granddaughter and her husband produced an award-winning 90-minute documentary about her called *Big Sonia*. The film interweaves Sonia's past of survival and the present of a woman who can barely see over the steering wheel of her 1989 beige Oldsmobile 98, yet insists on driving herself to work every day to run her late husband's tailor shop, John's Tailoring. The film has been shown all around the world, including in China, Israel, Germany, and Poland. There have been more than 200 screenings in movie theaters and communities, and a 45-minute educational version has been shown in dozens of schools, prisons, and organizations. Sonia and her eldest daughter, Regina Kort, often speak together about Sonia's Holocaust experience in front of audiences large and small, addressing the dangers and lessons of hate. Her secret to a life well lived is getting up to go to work every day and the boost that the notoriety and purpose

Big Sonia has given her. The movie is now part of the Library of Congress and, in 2018, there was a special screening of the documentary before the House of Representatives. *Big Sonia* qualified for an Academy Award and has won 25 awards to date.

Other examples abound. Barbara met two remarkable older women in a class she took four years ago. One impressed her with her travels to pursue her photography career while caring for her elderly husband, who has exhibited signs of dementia. Margaret has a friend in her late 60s who lived alone and valiantly fought for several years a rare form of breast cancer that spread to other parts of her body while she continued to work as a newspaper journalist, sing in her church choir, and travel the world, until it was no longer feasible.

We also admire those we don't know but read and hear about, such as the late Supreme Court Justice Ruth Bader Ginsburg, who died at age 87. The *AARP Bulletin* featured a question-and-answer piece by Hugh Delehanty with Twyla Tharp, the choreographer now in her late 70s, who still dances with modifications. When asked, "What is the biggest misconception about aging?" she replied, "That it becomes less than what it once was rather than just the opposite: an accumulation of knowledge and experience and options. As we get older, there are more options, not fewer."[1]

What we've taken from these age-defiers is that the older years are not a time to cease to live—despite all the ailments, illnesses, and gray hairs that can be a part of the process. Each birthday may be tougher to acknowledge but is important to celebrate with gusto and with cake, ice cream, and candles.

Time is of the essence. We are on the clock with dwindling months and years ahead. More important, we must savor each day by waking up with a sense of gratitude. Barbara tries to meditate before getting into her daily routine of coffee, newspaper, work, and exercise. She took a weekly watercolor painting class before the pandemic of 2020 put a stop to it. Margaret listens to 30 minutes of classical music or opera to chill before she gets out of bed and then tries to walk outside most days for at least 30 minutes. When the weather is bad, she takes an in-place power walk in her living room along with a YouTube video, which she began using when the coronavirus pandemic of 2020 hit New York City. She continues to tutor and mentor underserved kids, which she did virtually during the pandemic, an activity that's the sweet spot in her life.

Each day we try to move forward rather than look back. We avoid dwelling on regrets, even though we each have some. We decided that the best way to embrace the older years is by accepting our current state as the new normal and periodically adjusting what we must do to maintain our optimism. Here's how that translates into real-world tips:

Stop worrying about the small stuff. Keep worries in perspective to avoid them escalating and taking on a life of their own. How do we counteract sadness when not invited to the wedding of a friend's daughter when we expected to make the cut? Close friends and our inner voices remind us that we have no control over these matters. That isn't to say they don't weigh us down. If and when they do, we try to reduce stress by taking a walk and clearing our head, venting to a good friend, practicing meditation or yoga, or reading a book to escape. We have learned to focus most on what we can control.

Zero in on assets, not deficits. Consciously try to remember what we have to be thankful for and build on that. Our assets can be easily forgotten or taken for granted—loved ones, dear friends, home, work, health, education, prior travels. It's about our accomplishments and the joy we get from seeing others succeed at something. Margaret feels she is lucky to have worked with some amazing underserved kids and their families, which continues to change her perspective on life. She frequently notes that she gets much more out of it than the kids do. She's also met wonderful women in the process.

Even if Barbara never gets to travel again, she happily remembers all the places she's been. Barbara fondly recalls a trip to Switzerland to study French when she was 12 years old, visiting charming towns amid mountains, seeing the majestic Matterhorn in Zermatt reached by a cog railroad train, and eating gooey fondue and dark chocolate. She hopes to return but knows that, if she can't, she retains the memories.

If you doubt that you're fortunate, make a list, add one good thing each day, and keep it in a file on your computer, in note mode on your phone, or on a yellow-lined pad. Reread it when you feel a pity party looming.

Keep learning to recharge or exercise the brain. Expand your knowledge about what you know or, better yet, tackle a new topic. Try a new type of cooking—Mexican or Indian or Turkish cuisine. Take up a new instrument or tune your piano and see if you remember chords and keys. Learn how to play bridge or do crossword or jigsaw puzzles. Beef up your technology chops. Join a study group in your community or house of worship; maybe it's time to start reading mysteries, science fiction, or memoirs. Sign up for a lecture or movie series and learn from the experts. Take an art or photography class. With the list of online classes, lectures, and concerts that exploded during the COVID-19 pandemic of 2020, you don't have to spend big bucks or even leave the comfort of your home to learn something new.

Like exercise but bored with your routine of walking on a treadmill or performing yoga poses a few times a week? Change it up. Take Pilates or try barre work. Not too long ago, nine out of 10 new apartment buildings were constructed with a gym, which shows the importance of wellness and fitness in daily life. You don't have to be a crazy warrior and run a 5K. Move, learn, and work hands and feet. It's also good for your brain. Not all exercise has to cost money. Apps and many online options are free.

Notice the world around you more. It's damn amazing, the scenery and people in it—if you take the time to notice it. Again, get out and take a walk down a new street for fresh air, sky, clouds, foliage, and big views. As Karen Duffy writes in her book, *Backbone: An Inspirational Manual for Coping with Chronic Pain*, chronic pain can make you become a *flâneur* (a wanderer). Walking is the best exercise for many reasons: it's cheap, easy, and harmless, requires only a good pair of athletic shoes, is good for your lungs and your heart, enables you to really take in the sights and sounds around you, and can be solitary or done with others. Walk indoors at a museum and look at the art. Margaret has discovered so many different neighborhoods in her new Manhattan borough. She still wants to explore the other boroughs of the Bronx, Brooklyn, Queens, and Staten Island.

Consider adding in spontaneity. We like writer Heidi Herman's idea of "planned spontaneity" in her book about how her mother navigated her older years well, *On with the Butter! Spread More Living onto Everyday Life*. Herman thought of her Mom as a life adventurer and wrote, "She taught me to embrace life with exuberance and did so well into her 90s." Although it may sound contrary to those of us who schedule almost everything we do, Herman suggests slipping into one's day some spur-of-the-moment possibilities. "For example," she writes, "if it will take 10 minutes to pick up your library books, plan 30 minutes or even an hour just in case something is happening when you get there."[2] Perhaps you'll chat with a stranger or spend more time scanning shelves for the latest best sellers. We probably will still plan but now try to have some time for those just-in-case moments that might put more bounce in our steps on any given day.

Get enough sleep. Nancy H. Rothstein, The Sleep Ambassador®, emphasizes the importance of sleep: Getting good sleep is essential for good days as well as for your physical and mental health. Chronic sleep deprivation or an untreated sleep disorder can lead to myriad health risks including cardiovascular disease, depression, and early onset dementia. Insufficient sleep can also lower your sex drive (at this age you may ask, "What sex drive?" but you can deal with that later), weaken your immune system, wreak havoc on your memory, and lead to weight gain. Rothstein also advocates turning off all screens, which means TVs, phones, and tablets, at least one hour before bedtime so you can transition to sleep in peace.

Make a new friend or ignite a romance or both. A relative once told Barbara that "We don't make friends at our age (in our 70s)." *Hogwash*, thought Barbara. Circumstances to meet new people regularly present themselves. The glitch is that it often involves getting off your ass and out the door. Nervous? We have been there, too, but we're used to asking questions of people we hardly know. In social circumstances, we try to dial down our inquisitiveness. Since Margaret moved to New York City in 2019, she tries to speak to someone new each day. She'll say "hello" and ask about their lives: where they're headed if she meets them on a bus or the subway or what they're cooking if she meets them in a long grocery line. Barbara has made close friends while having a pedicure and attending a dinner orchestrated by a store in her village.

Meeting and reconnecting with old friends is another option. Class reunions may be dreaded rituals for some, yet we have found they can be a rich source of new friendships. Or, get reacquainted with former friends with whom you've lost touch, which many people did during the COVID-19 pandemic of 2020.

Speaking of touch, we all need it from time to time, whether in a relationship with a partner, getting a massage, or having your hair washed at a salon. Sex, by the way, is a healthy endeavor and can prolong life. Not dating? Ask a friend to fix you up, pay a professional matchmaker, or go online to one of the many dating sites. And don't rule out all those exciting new vibrators, and other sex toys. Their sales soared during the pandemic.

Embrace others by entertaining at home. So few do it as they age, thinking it's so much work and expense. Keep it easy if you're fearful or busy. Do takeout (if informal, order pizzas), or cook simple, one-sheet or one-pot recipes, two trends in many new cookbooks and food blogs. Use glasses, plates, and cutlery that you can put in your dishwasher rather than hand wash.

For those a bit more adventuresome, we anticipate the return of dinner parties post-COVID-19 pandemic of 2020—especially since so many people took up or improved their cooking chops while staying at home. Some friends we know turned into competitors for the likes of Ina (Garten), Mashama (Bailey), Deb (Perelman), and other food pros.

Get regular checkups to stay healthy. Tune up your body. We're big advocates of having our bodies checked annually or more often, just as we have our furnaces inspected and cleaned yearly. This includes checking vision for glaucoma, macular degeneration, and cataracts; getting an annual mammogram and pap smear; and having a hearing test for a baseline and then getting that checked regularly. People who cannot hear others' conversations often turn inward and experience depression. Despite the expense, hearing aids today are barely noticeable and employ better technology.

Visit your internist at least once a year for a check of vitals such as blood pressure and cholesterol. Barbara requires quarterly doctor visits because of certain conditions. We both have a colonoscopy every five years or so, depending on results and family history. We visit our ob-gyns for urinary tract infections that are common among aging women. Margaret goes to an endocrinologist once a year for a bone density test and to a dermatologist for an annual freckle check.

We also are diligent with our visits to the dentist. Barbara goes quarterly for cleanings. In between we brush, floss, and rinse twice or three times daily. And we get an annual flu vaccine and pneumonia shot and have had the two-part shingle shots. We eagerly awaited a coronavirus vaccination.

We urge our male friends and loved ones to have regular checkups for their prostates, PSA tests, cholesterol, blood pressure, and other conditions.

Don't forget medical insurance. After age 65, what's available for many is good health insurance from Medicare and supplemental health and drug plans. For us, they have been lifelines. They're not free, but these are at the top of our budget priority list. Having these plans in place helps us to afford to nip a problem in the bud before it worsens, whether polyps found during a colonoscopy or cysts found during a pelvic exam. Physician Atul Gawande wrote about keeping track of what to do with health and other challenges in *The Checklist Manifesto: How to Get Things Right.*

Get emotional tune-ups. Feeling blah or down? Loneliness can lead to feelings of sadness with more of life behind us than ahead of us, especially when we remember friends who are ill or have died. Regular anxiety may surface, as well as depression, which often occurs in old age, and permeated more lives during the COVID-19 pandemic of 2020. Meds to boost serotonin may be called for. Exercise also works wonders. Psychotherapy need not be expensive, and many therapists take some form of insurance. Support groups, often free, can also be a boon. Even some periodic anxiety might be a good reason to see a mental health professional, which is what Barbara did a few times when she grew concerned about her mother's failing health. As Margaret reminded her, "Good therapy is a sign of strength."

Develop a new healthy routine. You're not too old to mix things up, but tackle one step at a time, whether it relates to eating, exercising, sleeping, or hygiene. Try doing it the same time every day. On average, it's said to take more than two months before a new behavior becomes automatic—66 days to be exact, according to Phillipa Lally et al.'s study at University College London, published in the *European Journal of Social Psychology.*[3] Even more good news is that making a mistake once or twice has no measurable impact on long-term goals, says James Clear, author of *Atomic Habits.* So, don't worry if you forget to floss occasionally—it's ok as long as you keep it up over the long haul.

Get legal expertise to protect yourself and those you love most. That means spending some money to have legal documents for your heirs drawn up for you or doing it yourself online (there are good options available) such as drafting a will, trust, and health proxy. Don't want to be resuscitated or intubated? Sign a living will that stipulates this.

Shore up your finances. Cut back on expenses if you live on a fixed income, which many of us do. Maybe you don't still need to drive. Sell your car (or, if you have two, get rid of one). Instead, walk, do ride-shares, or take public transportation. Not having a car eliminates the costs of repairs, gasoline, and insurance. Also, pay down debt if you can: High credit card balances result in expensive interest rates that just dig deeper debt holes. Pay off your mortgage if you have one and can do so. You might refinance your home and use the cash savings to do so. Bag the expensive trip and take a mini-vacation close to home. Don't promise to give your grown child money to help buy a car; now is the time for them to assert their financial independence. Consider renting out a room or your home for income if your building or town permits. Suze Orman, in an article in the *AARP Bulletin*, "Your 2020 Smart Money Action Plan," maps out 10 "moves to secure your future, which include considering Roth accounts and long-term care insurance."[4]

Avoid scams that target older folks. There are always unscrupulous people who look for the most vulnerable to bilk them out of their money, especially older folks who often are the most naïve. Someone who sounds sincere over the phone calls and pretends to be from Social Security, the Internal Revenue Service (IRS), or another governmental office—and the next thing you know, your bank account is drained. Older Americans lose roughly $3 billion to fraud each year, according to the U.S. Senate Special Committee on Aging, reported in 2019 and cited in an *AARP Bulletin*'s article on fraud.[5]

To avoid scams, never share personal information over the phone or Internet, and never give strangers access to your home. If suspicious, call the company and ask if it dispatched someone to your house. If you suspect a scam email, fill out a form at ic3.org, an Internet crime complaint center that collects scam emails to avoid scamming. Use nomorobo.com to block scammers on your landline (it's free) or on your cell (a small fee).

If you're a victim of a scam or suspicious that one is happening, call 911 or the non-emergency number for police to report the scam. Contact the three credit agencies, put a fraud alert on your account, and freeze your credit. Check your credit report at least once a year; we all get one free report annually. If you're a victim of identity theft, contact the Federal Trade Commission. Also, you might consider signing up for LifeLock, an American theft protection company that monitors for identity theft, the use of your personal information, and credit score changes. Monitor your checking account, check credit charges that aren't yours, and alert your bank or credit card company immediately.

Clean out your clutter so your heirs aren't stuck with the task. It's a great feeling of relief to declutter while you're alive. Make sure that whatever you keep of value is mentioned in your will as going to a designated person.

Know how to leverage technology. High-tech devices can make life easier, even if they sometimes require help to set them up and learn how to use them, says Lisa Cini, who is a resource for which devices, apps, and software to buy to age with independence (see the bibliography for her books). It's also good for the brain to learn something new. Perhaps you can set up Amazon Echo or learn to Zoom with loved ones.

Leave a good legacy. Accept the inevitable. Nobody gets to stay in this world forever. We all must depart—a swan song, adieu, bye-bye, it was great while it lasted. Do the work now to be sure you leave something good behind, which means teaching and loving family and friends and sometimes disagreeing with them rather than hoping to be everyone's best bud. Consider leaving funds—even a modest sum—for a cause you believe in or doing good deeds now that some will remember. While we're alive, we can make choices. If you want to leave a bequest, stipulate where you want the funds to go. This is good control from the grave.

If we're mentally and physically healthy, the present is the time to enjoy the quietness of being or plunging in and trying something new and maybe wild before it's too late. It's up to us and will be reflected in the decisions we make.

Chapter Three

Persons of Interest

Friendship

Margaret was sitting cross-legged in a living room chair reading about Harry and Meghan in a magazine article when the phone rang. It was Barbara. She was nervous about the results of a medical test that indicated she might need surgery and wanted a morale boost. Margaret listened to Barbara process the news out loud and tried not to interrupt or throw in her two cents. "I'm here for you," Margaret said.

Later, in a follow-up call, she assured Barbara. "This is hard. You've done hard things before. I'll help with whatever you need—doctors, where to go, whatever."

There were more ups and downs as Barbara gathered more information about the necessary procedure and her fear mounted. There were calls to Margaret early in the morning, and calls late at night. Barbara worried, "What if I'm going to die? Do you think I'll be okay?"

Margaret reminded Barbara that she is not Cassandra. However, she added her admiration for Barbara's strength, tenacity, and ability to research and find the best doctors, hospitals, and protocol. "You are good at controlling what you can."

Such intensity in any relationship—romantic or friendship—can be daunting. But it's a written understanding between the two of us that regardless of the circumstances, we will fill in for each other and offer an ear or hand unconditionally. However, we are not attached at the hip.

Are we best friends? We have what authors Aminatou Sow and Ann Friedman call a "Big Friendship" in their book: *How We Keep Each*

Other Close. They write, "Words like 'best friend' or BFF don't capture the adult emotional work we've put into this relationship. We now call it a *Big Friendship*, because it's one of the most affirming—and most complicated—relationships that a human life can hold."[1]

How well we know. Thirty-three years after writing our first book together on family business, *Corporate Bloodlines: The Future of the Family Firm*, we know that we make a good team. We have written together hundreds of articles, 10 books, hundreds of weekly blogs for our website, and given dozens of interviews and speeches. We know how the other thinks, finish each other's sentences, and interrupt each other routinely. We got through the 2020 coronavirus pandemic, in part, because we could complain, without apology, about feeling trapped indoors, as well as angry about people who didn't wear masks, wash their hands, or maintain their physical distance. We have become the equivalent of an old married couple, though we rarely bicker.

Daily, even on most weekends, we talk business. We also laugh and cry and share some of the most exciting news and most private and worst stories we could tell about ourselves. We both know how important our friendship is as a form of sustenance, especially after we each lost a spouse. However, as close as we are, we each have dozens of other close friends. Most important, we trust the other to keep our secrets like a sphinx. If we hurt one another's feelings, never meaning to, we apologize and work on maintaining the friendship. Friends are supposed to do that, we believe, and we always have.

Friendship is not just fluffy stuff good for anecdotes. Friendship is almost as important to us as breathing oxygen. In many cases, it is our oxygen, representing a basic human need along with food, sleep, and safety to help us stay alive, thrive, and grow. Studies have shown that social isolation and loneliness can be harmful, resulting in emotional and physical downsides and early death. Even in the animal kingdom, friendships are imperative.

Lydia Denworth writes in her book, *Friendship: The Evolution, Biology, and Extraordinary Power of Life's Fundamental Bond*, that she sees the urge to connect reflected in primates. That, she says, offers insight into human social bonds. She takes readers to a monkey sanctuary in Puerto Rico and a baboon colony in Kenya to examine animal bonds. She asks what friends are for. She also poses that question to her son Jake about his best friend growing up. His response: "I can't think of anyone I like more."[2]

Friends are the family we choose. If we're sick, they help us heal, maybe bringing over chicken soup. If we're not contagious, they might even feed it to us. Friends also gossip, make us laugh, fill out our table on holidays, and take us to the doctor if we need a procedure like a colonoscopy or cataract surgery. They help us move, decorate, cook, celebrate marriages and births, and serve as a source of comfort when life presents challenges.

When Margaret's husband died, Barbara called daily. She remembered Margaret's first anniversary without her husband with a bouquet of flowers. When Barbara's husband walked out, Margaret hosted a surprise birthday cocktail dinner at a restaurant. When a childhood friend asked Barbara to help her after an operation, Barbara flew to her home to grocery shop, cook, do errands, and keep her company. Margaret had a friend whose husband was diagnosed with an illness. She needed to talk to the doctor and asked Margaret to hold her hand, which meant accompany her to the hospital, ask questions, listen, and take notes.

Friends help forestall loneliness. According to a 2018 online poll of 20,000 people conducted by insurance giant Cigna, nearly half of Americans reported sometimes or always feeling lonely, which is different from being on your own or alone. There are even scientists who study this phenomenon. Loneliness researcher John Cacioppo, cited in Denworth's book, believes that the feeling is akin to hunger and is an adaptive response to let us know that it's time to be with others, just as our stomach growling signals that we need to eat.[3] During the CO-VID-19 pandemic of 2020, when we sheltered inside our homes, and then very tentatively outside our homes, often alone or with a spouse, partner, or children, we found that reaching out to close friends through FaceTime, Zoom, phone calls, emails, and texts helped us feel less lonely and anxious.

How do we select friends? Is friendship a matter of chemistry the way romantic relationships are? In an article in the *New York Times*, "You Share Everything with Your Bestie. Even Brain Waves." (April 16, 2018), science writer Natalie Angier addresses why we're attracted to certain people based on our hardwiring. Carolyn Parkinson, a cognitive scientist at the University of California, Los Angeles, told her, "I was struck by the exceptional magnitude of similarity among friends." The results "were more persuasive than I would have thought."[4]

Generally, friendships aren't stagnant but ramp up and down across life stages. Most of our first friendships started in childhood. Maybe we met at a playground or in a grade school class. Perhaps we took ballet together, lived next door, got to know one another's families, and read together. On weekends, we slept at each other's houses, talked about boys, and analyzed friends. Or we ice skated, went to the movies, studied together, rode bikes, attended the same dances, and participated in each other's weddings.

We also would hang out at each other's houses. Margaret's household was a noisy one and she'd go over to her friends' homes to chill. Her best friend's home housed a quiet family of calm, bookish people. Margaret brought noise and a certain energy like jokes, fierce opinions, and a big laugh. Her friend's parents did not mind having her disturb their peace in this way. The calmness of their lives soothed Margaret.

Margaret and her bestie knew almost everything about each other: collections, hobbies, shoes, hairstyles, clothing they liked, and who were their latest likes and loves. They played the same board games, read some of the same books and magazines, went swimming together, loved the same foods, especially one restaurant's hamburgers and fries, and relished cooking and experimenting with recipes. Of course, like most close friends, they had separate interests. Their friendship spans 66 years.

Barbara has remained close with her longest-time friend of 68 years. Her friend instructed her not to say she's her oldest friend, which implies years rather than depth. They lived next door in suburban homes, strung tin cans together across their properties to pretend they were talking by phone (there were only landlines back then), baked chocolate chip cookies—once with too much salt instead of sugar—and ran through sprinklers on hot summer days. By the time we hit middle and high school, some of us had a larger pool of friends. Two friends Margaret made in middle school were smart, passionate, well-read, and funny. Barbara forged new bonds in high school and through camp and other summer programs. She found it liberating to move on to a wider pool after going to a small K–8 grade school.

Some of those early friendships offer Barbara and Margaret great sustenance today and became part of regular Zoom groups during the coronavirus pandemic of 2020. These are the folks who knew them well and shared important history about each other's parents, siblings, teachers, and houses, plus dysfunction that ran through their family lives and the era's silence about many important issues, from affairs to divorces, homosexuality, gender identity, race, and religion.

We went off to college and met people in our dorms, classes, and activities. We were assigned a roommate. Sometimes it was a match, other times not. Margaret had an instant friendship with one roomie who was an art major from a small town. They were quite different but bonded over their passion for Beach Boys records. They double-dated, protested the Vietnam War, washed their hair together on Friday afternoons, then did their nails. Years later, although in different cities, they kept in touch, still reminiscing about the time they both got served in a bar (although underage), drank too much beer, and got sick, both of them rushing to beat the other to the bathroom. Each time they'd talk, the reminiscing became embellished and funnier. As William Faulkner said, "The past is never dead. It's not even past."

For Barbara, college at two women's schools brought forth new types of friends. Many were not Jewish—her religion and that of most of her friends growing up in her suburban New York bubble. They came from different parts of the country, which was eye-opening, including one Midwestern friend who dated a very "successful" drug-pusher at a then prestigious all-male university. She distinctly remembers finding friends who lived much less sheltered lives, coming from divorced homes and homes with addiction, domestic violence, and other kinds of abuse. Many were from low-income families so they were on scholarships and worked in college. Some had different political views as the Vietnam War ramped up.

As we moved on from college to our careers and possibly marriage, the process by which we chose friends changed again. We met them at work, in our neighborhoods, apartment buildings, on our suburban blocks, or through our children, if we had them. Some became couple friends.

In most cases, they admired us. We admired them. They made us laugh, feel good, and challenged us intellectually. We were similar ages, had similar lives, or similar hobbies and interests—kids, pets, music, theater, art, and various collections. Barbara remembers the fun of taking cooking classes with several friends, sharing New Year's Eve lobster dinners, and working in interesting journalism jobs at a monthly magazine, daily newspaper, and national trade association. At each, teamwork was essential and deep bonds were forged. She keeps up with several who remember when print journalism meant using electric typewriters, lined "copy" paper with carbons, counting characters, and watching type set. Margaret remembers the same and is still friendly with the editor and someone she worked with on a Jewish community newspaper in the late 60s/early 70s. She has gone out for occasional lunches with staff who are still around.

In middle age, we kept some friends we met throughout our lives but started to make new ones with similar accomplishments and values. And when we got together, whether one on one or in groups of women, we talked about cooking, travels, books, movies, and politics. As couples, we gave dinner parties where the two of us each liked debating issues of the day: social justice and politics, finance, investments, books, movies, travel, and, of course, food and wine.

Perhaps we were part of the same team at work or met on a trip. Margaret and her husband Nolan were traveling to Bermuda and sat on the plane next to a couple they had never met whose son, they discovered, was friendly with their younger son in high school. The two couples spent every day and night on that trip together.

The friendship continued after they returned home. When Nolan died, this couple was there for her. They were an anchor. Barbara feels fortunate to have a strong network of later-life friends—one from a 40th high school reunion who never was a friend back then. "I don't think we ever talked," she says, and they now try to talk several times a week. She met others she cherishes, detecting a clue that they might be a good match. Maybe they seemed energetic, funny, smart, empathetic, non-cliquey, or open to sharing life rather than maintaining a tight façade.

Why do we put so much stock in new friendships? As we've aged, our kids have moved out (we hope) and on to their own busy lives and families, and we realize we've lost not just spouses but friends to death and to other circumstances. We've evolved and so have they, and we no longer are always simpatico with everyone.

We are not willing to continue in relationships that are high maintenance and grow toxic. We don't shed friends lightly but know that our mental well-being may make it necessary. As we know, some friendships can be fragile. "In one of the few studies of long-term friendships, researchers surveyed hundreds of adults and found that only 30 percent of their closest friends still remained close after seven years," say Aminatou and Friedman in their book.[5] We also know it's important to make new friends. We've been able to do so by putting in more work than just Facebook-friending one or buying one, we joke, on eBay or Craigslist. Our computer screens are not our front door. *Au contraire.*

To meet new people, we get out and are open to the possibility. Much like we found with dating, no one, we know, is going to knock on our doors. We seek out new folks, social circles, and communities. We've recognized that as we age and more of our loved ones pass away, one of the best new places to meet new people over age 60 can be, sadly, at shivas, wakes, and funerals.

Regardless of where we meet and how, opening ourselves up to strangers makes us vulnerable. Some will rebuff us even as we ask a second or third time, "Would you like to grab coffee (wine or lunch)?" Dead silence or changing the conversation hurts. We've learned to move on.

Here's a sample of what we've done to connect. One afternoon Margaret met a nattily dressed man on the subway. She began the conversation by complimenting him on his tie. From there she learned that he was a social worker who helped kids in the foster care system get adopted and was writing a book about the African diaspora. They chatted about writing until she got off the train. They shook hands and hoped they would run into each other again. He gave her his business card. These are what we call "pop-up friendships." Margaret's younger sister met her husband on an airplane more than three decades ago. Sometimes it takes extra work to email or call and spend more time together.

Barbara made friends with one couple on a trip to China with her mother. She met a couple at an impromptu dinner party hosted by a store in their Upstate New York area. After running into them a few more times, she invited them to her home for a party. She made a younger friend when taking a *plein air* painting workshop with her. When Barbara moved back East 10 years ago to a village where she knew nobody, she discovered the joy of a woman reaching out to her. Part of a duo who owned a store, the woman asked Barbara about herself, then said, "I know we'll be friends. Come with me to my temple." Our stories connect us.

There are many other ways to make new friends:

1. At an event. Example: If you're a member of your local art museum and there's an event for friends, go. You never know who'll you'll meet.
2. At a subway or bus stop, a bookstore, or book group, standing in line at a grocery store or pharmacy, sitting at the bar in a restaurant, through volunteer work, at your library or place of worship, or through community organizations such as senior centers, YMCAs, and gyms.

3. In a class. Barbara has made several friends in her Pilates, Jewish, and painting classes. Margaret has befriended a group of women with whom she tutored in Harlem. She also met someone at physical therapy and when doing a project for the homeless during Christmas. When she started Pilates, she met women who lunched after class. They asked her to join them.
4. Through invitations you extend. Invite neighbors over to get to know them. Perhaps they can become friends, too, or might have people they'd like to introduce you to.
5. Go back to the well. Reconnect with former friends at a class reunion as both Barbara and Margaret have done. After Margaret's 50th high school reunion, a group of women, all of whom went to grade school together, started having brunch on Sundays on a regular basis. Margaret engineered their get togethers. At a high school reunion, Barbara became close with a widower who lived a block away. They never talked back then, but now they regularly do, and Barbara organized a birthday dinner for his 70th with other mutual friends. Barbara likes going to her beau's school reunions. So many friends asked, "Why would you do that?" "Simple," she has replied, "I want to fill in the holes in his past that I didn't know about and meet his friends."
6. From your service contacts. Some people become friendly with their hairdresser, manicurist, or trainer. Barbara now socializes with her trainer and her husband and has invited over an employee of a store she frequents who seemed eager to extend her network. Add in your yoga instructor, doctor, lawyer, or morning barista. If you see them enough times and schmooze, you might say that you'd like to get to know them better.

Not all friendships are created equal. Why are some people we meet close friends and others mere acquaintances? We make an acquaintance of someone we don't see that often. They're fun but someone with whom we don't feel the urge to become close. Regardless, acquaintances still expand our worldview, especially those who have different experiences and talents than we do. Discovering that your friend down the street is an opera singer or is into bird watching adds a new dimension to the conversation and to your life. Barbara made three close friends at a religious education class and considers others who were in attendance acquaintances. Margaret met someone in New York City whom she considers to be an acquaintance. She is a great resource for doctors, restaurants, and more. What bonds the closer-knit ones is tough to define but she thinks they simply share similar values, curiosity, humor, and an openness to making new friends.

At the same time, we depend on our close circle to meet different needs, especially challenges. Scientists have found that the brains of close friends respond in remarkably similar ways. According to Angier's "Wired to Be Besties" article, our friends are often much like us—it's tribal. We share similar connections of age, race, religion, values, socioeconomic status, educational level, political leaning, and more. In today's parlance, they "just get us." Other times, they vary, but we so admire them, and they return the compliment. However, now that we're older and wiser, we're more willing to move out of our comfort zone to connect with different types of people. Margaret met a woman with whom she became friendly while doing a mentoring project. Their lives were vastly different, but they bonded over learning, a love of cooking, and their passion for working with young people.

We each found that now is a great time to expand our relationships to make life richer, especially with those of different ages. We like that mix and match approach. The young friends keep us abreast of pop culture, new technology, food trends, and raising children today, while the older ones share their years of wisdom, experience, and stories. We called Barbara's mother the Jewish *Scheherazade*. A few years back, Barbara began sharing her with two of her childhood friends who regularly gathered at her home. They had lost their mothers and treasured having Barbara's mother to tell what it was like growing up in their suburban village as well as what it was like to age. It kept Barbara's mother involved since she had lost so many friends. Everyone enjoyed the interplay until she could no longer join them.

How do you know if there's a connection when you meet someone new or renew an old relationship?

We have posed these questions to ourselves:

- Do you both seem to enjoy each other's company enough to keep the conversation lively and engaging?
- Do you look forward to getting together each time—or not? And if you agree to get together, do you enjoy their company even more the second or third time? If not, perhaps this is not a match.

- Is this someone you can imagine confiding in and sharing advice and ideas with, or is it merely superficial? For example, you might see them occasionally to discuss movies because they're a buff.
- Does this person fit into your gal pal circle of friendships and vice versa? It's so much fun to get together as a group, schmoozing, laughing, discussing movies, books, politics, gossiping, playing cards, sipping wine, breaking bread, and sharing stories.
- Does the person make you feel good? If so, that can be reason enough, but know that not everybody fits into a mold.

Always bear in mind that however you make new friends, important relationships need to be nurtured to thrive and last. They feed on time, love, attention, and trust. Yet, as we age and get busy, downsize, and move away or take a different path, friendships fluctuate, evolve, and fizzle. Take time to preserve those most important to you. Pick up the phone, send an email or text, write an old-fashioned letter, or call. "Thinking of you" is sometimes all you must say to start. Many reached out during the COVID-19 pandemic of 2020, fearful long-time friends had gotten sick or died.

Eventually, Margaret's friendship with her college roomie burned out because they really didn't have enough in common after each married and lived in different cities. They had vastly different husbands, careers, parenting styles, and values. This is typical as we go through passages in our lives. Interests and values change, people move away, or date or marry someone we don't like, which can drive a wedge between old friends. Expectations may not be the same.

One friend of Barbara's worried that their strong bond was unraveling and asked her if their friendship was worth saving. Barbara was surprised that her friend felt it had gotten to that point. The friends emailed, talked, and got through their blip. Each took responsibility. Barbara felt she was more at fault because of extenuating family circumstances. She has subsequently worked hard not to have it happen again. All friendships have some strife. Aminatou and Friedman say they went to couple's therapy when their friendship hit a big bump.

Yet, some friendships still shatter like priceless porcelain that cannot be put back together, no matter how much we try. Was it a nasty comment that caused the rift? An unsympathetic response to a personal issue?

Friends can split up over money and even splitting a bill. However a friendship dissolves, it can be about "a cruel thing said or outrageous thing done—that supremely tellable violation usually is the climax to frustrations and disappointments that had been building over time," say Aminatou and Friedman.

Barbara has lost a few friendships. One friend resented her for not using her real estate services to sell a home. Another ghosted her, or stopped replying, for reasons Barbara could not discern. Barbara tried multiple times, then gave up, yet still wonders what "sin" she committed 35 years ago. She also cut the cord with one friend whose high-maintenance needs she felt she could never meet. Barbara decided it was best to accept that the friendship had run its course. Now older, we move on with greater resiliency.

And then, sometimes, we say or do the wrong thing. We mean well but it comes off as snarky or uncaring when the underlying idea was compassion with perhaps misplaced humor. There are also situations where friends do not show up when we need them—perhaps when we've had a serious illness or loss. Often there is no agenda other than the fact that they aren't sure what to say or how to react. So, they keep silent, which can be interpreted as not caring. When trauma strikes, it can be disconcerting to find that the friends you thought you had aren't there for you. We have a friend whose husband is ill who said to us, "There were women who I thought were my friends. They disappeared."

If we value the friendship, we work harder to make amends. The cliché that life is short remains germane. The point is that we've reached a time in our lives where we don't want to hold ourselves back or have a regret. Some friendships become stronger, others still die.

Reasons why friendships may end:

- Too self-focused. Everything is about her (or him).
- Too uncaring. The friend never or rarely initiates contact but waits for you to do so.
- Selfish. The friend never shares friends but latches onto yours and initiates contact with your friends without including you.
- Judgmental. The person finds fault with you to a degree that makes you feel uncomfortable when together.
- Boss lady. The friend frequently tells you what you should be doing in a tone that doesn't reflect your needs.

- Bad listener. The friend always talks and rarely listens to what you need to say or explain and sometimes takes all the air out of the room.
- Uncomplimentary. The friend never tells you she likes your hair, outfit, cooking, or anything. Who needs that?
- Forgetful. The friend doesn't care about your milestone events. No cards, calls gifts, or emails. Moreover, she's surprised that you remember hers. Duh, it's not that hard. Put it into your smartphone.
- Never forgets. Perhaps you unwittingly, to be glib, said something that offended. You apologize and remain friends. However, she works your *faux pas* into a conversation almost every time you're together.
- Doesn't have your back. When someone criticizes you, the friend isn't there to stick up for you.
- Different values. A difference or two is fine—even good, since our friends should be peas from different pods. However, many differences and strong opinions about yours is not okay. Or, you may have grown apart. Time to move on and remember fondly the good parts.
- Too much distance. Sometimes a lack of proximity causes each person to drift away, without any confrontation or palpable reason. However, that doesn't preclude staying in touch through social media, cards, and an occasional phone call, email, or text.
- The ultimate farewell. As we age, we lose friends through sickness and death, but we may choose to remain in touch with their families.

A significant friendship with decades of history can sprinkle magic into our lives. "When you find a Big Friendship, hold on to it. Invest in it. Stretch for it," say Aminatou and Friedman. At the same time, we're open to new potential friends and believe it's never too late to form a bond and love of a different kind than the romantic type. The reason is simple. Friendships can be a treasure you can't buy at any store but whose gifts resonate deep within our hearts.

Chapter Four

Do You Really Want an Old Geezer?

A Look at Who's Left on the Shelf

It's a warm spring evening. You're on your second date with a man you met through friends. You walk and talk. You feel a strong connection. He turns to you and says, "I believe I have to kiss you." He holds you by the shoulders and kisses you on the lips. He kisses you and kisses you. You kiss back. You are limp. Your knees feel like Jell-O.

"Let's go to my apartment," he suggests.

You joke, in your slightly prudish tone, "Then you won't have any respect for me." However, you're really thinking, "I don't want him to see my flabby body and stretch marks."

You're also aware that if you don't have sex with him, he most likely won't call you again with so many chicks available. Sex. That's what many of these men really want even at this age. You know because you've been on a few first dates that were a bust. There was no way you were going to kiss let alone sleep with any of them. Yet, you now know that this is all part of the deal if you want to become a duo at an advanced age. These aging paramours still have strong libidos.

With this guy, you feel sexy, attractive, and sense the beginning of that illusive magic called chemistry. You rationalize that it's worth it to have the companionship, sex, and intimacy at your age, sort of a now or never attitude.

You go to his apartment. He puts his arms around you. It feels so good. You undress, preferring to do so in the dark. The sex is slow but good. When you connect, there is a deep shiver. This is not a quick,

33

detached sexual foray or sex for having children. It's about some deep longing to connect and to be fulfilled. Afterward, you even laugh.

You spend the rest of that year together. You amble and stroll through parks. Late at night, you listen to jazz and drink wine, go to classical music concerts, opera, theater, museums, and baseball games. You glow, and friends comment. You are happy. You're part of a couple. You meet his family. He meets yours.

You know he's no Harrison Ford but hey, you're attracted to him, and you're not exactly Diane Keaton. He's also smart, funny, and kind. So what if he has a few health issues. So what if he has hair in some of the wrong places, isn't a chic dresser, doesn't have perfect teeth, and struggles to have an erection.

You also know that you need a sense of humor as you notice out of the corner of your eye his bottle of blue pills on the nightstand that make sex possible. When you get under the covers together, he reaches over—not to grab you—but to put on his Jacques Cousteau-like sleep machine mask to help him cope with his intense snoring and sleep apnea. In a moment of levity, you say, "Have a good dive, dear."

* * * * *

Who doesn't love the idea of holding hands, kissing, and enjoying good intimacy? Just because we're older and single doesn't mean we don't relish a relationship—and, yes, sex. We're not alone. If this weren't the case, there wouldn't be so many advertisements for medications—Viagra, Cialis, Stendra—for men to reverse erectile dysfunction by enhancing the effects of nitric oxide. To get clinical, that's the substance needed for the muscles in the penis to relax and allow chambers within to fill with blood, so it can become erect and hard.

Women, too, need their creams and gels to lubricate their vulva and vagina as it becomes dry and prune-like during post-menopause. It helps the penis to penetrate and not cause the woman pain. There's a reason so many women learned to say, "Not tonight, dear. I have a headache," rather than a vulva or vagina ache.

It's great to have remedies, but there's another vexing problem. Before we can have sexual intimacy, we need an honest live person, not one of those pretend boyfriends or girlfriends that help you deflect attention from being single. However, it's difficult to find available people to love romantically in our sixth, seventh, and eighth decades.

We affectionately refer to them as "old geezers," and they might call us "old bags." We don't mean to be disrespectful and hope they don't, either. The dictionary definition is not terribly flattering. An old geezer is an older person, especially one who is no longer cool or hip. It conjures up images of "grumpy old men" like Jack Lemmon and Walter Matthau played in the 1983 movie by the same title. For us, it's a way to put older guys into one category. And just so we don't sound sexist, both men and women have older-age issues such as thinning skin, turkey necks, and emotional baggage.

For heterosexual women, the challenge is to find the guys, which is tougher as we age. The same is true for gay women, especially over 50. Being a minority, it is of course much harder for gay folks to meet potential partners in more traditional ways—in their neighborhood, at parties, or at work. Online dating is an obvious way to increase the pool. Maria, a resident of California in her mid-50s, concurs. She finds it's difficult to meet women to date. Naturally, the COVID-19 pandemic of 2020 made it more of a challenge.

"Robert," 80, and "Edward," 67, met on Match. Within 30 minutes of their first meeting, the two men who live in St. Louis, Missouri, clicked. Both were surprised to learn that they lived only 1½ miles apart. If it hadn't been for online dating, the two most likely would never have connected.

If you're lucky, you might have friends fix you up, which happened to Barbara. A long-time friend met a college classmate at an annual gathering. The friend learned his classmate was single. He asked Barbara if she might be interested. She looked up his profile and thought why not. They talked and met at a charming French restaurant. It wasn't love at first bite for her; he says he was smitten from the start.

She gave him a second try, then a third, and remembers feeling extremely cautious after her divorce and online dating marathon. She wanted to take things slowly. Gradually, their relationship grew into a trifecta romance of companionship, caring, and cooking. "I equated him with a sweet onion. I kept peeling away layers as I learned about him, and he appealed more and more," she says.

Friends and even acquaintances went straight to the heart of the matter and asked, "Is there good chemistry?" She knew what they meant. "How's the sex?" Many pummeled her with additional questions. She often felt she was in a science experiment for older people who hadn't dated in decades and were curious what an older-age relationship entailed.

What friends asked:

- I heard you're dating. How serious is it? How'd you meet?
- How many nights each week do you spend together?
- How often do you see each other during the day?
- Do you stay at his place or yours?
- What's it like to be intimate at this age? Is it good or better?
- How do you get undressed in front of each other?
- Do you love each other, or is it just about companionship? Has he said he loves you? What have you told him?
- Might you live together?
- How do you share finances—do you split them or does he pick up the check all the time and if not, why? Who pays for what when you travel?
- Do you like his kids?
- Does he like your kids? What about your friends and family?
- Do you include each other at events you each are invited to?
- Have you shared your finances?
- He seems so different from your other partners.
- When can I/we meet him?
- Do you think you'll remarry?

Some questions she answered, many she didn't. As Barbara's relationship ramped up and she became part of a couple, she dubbed him her beau since boyfriend sounded too high-school-ish. She came to call him "Fixup" to maintain his privacy when she wrote about him. Although they remain a pair, they don't live under the same roof, which may be part of their success at this late stage when so many habits are fixed.

Those without a fixup possibility may connect with an old boyfriend or someone they had a crush on decades ago. They fantasize, "Wouldn't it be great to run into so and so again?" Perhaps, they meet at a reunion, sports event, or wine tasting where there's "opportunity," a code word for a healthy male population. Perhaps it happens on Facebook, Classmates.com, one of the dating sites, at a speed-dating gathering, or a political fundraiser. Margaret ran into a man at an Apple Store she had gone out with in high school more than 50 years ago. They reconnected and dated, finding that a former flame can be a familiar, safe, and comfortable way to find love. There's a shared history.

Maybe, at the time you dated, you were too young to be serious, or you both went off to different colleges and lost touch. Maybe, your family didn't approve of him, you came from different backgrounds and religions, which happened to a mutual friend of Margaret and Barbara, who's been happily remarried for decades to a man her father didn't approve of. No longer does this usually matter at our age. Time heals most wounds and differences, we've learned, especially when the male cohort is in such short supply. It's amazing how a slight paunch, balding head, and other common signs of aging count far less when older. We hope men cut us the same slack, though we know gray or white hair, extra pounds, and wrinkles don't appeal to all men, who sometimes find younger babes more alluring.

However, we become heartened when we see men in real life or on TV who show interest in women who exemplify a glamorous older persona like Helen Mirren or Angela Bassett. They're still gorgeous and sexy. Gina on the TV series *Delicious* appeals to several men in the show for her outgoing personality and fabulous cooking, and she doesn't turn them away because of her zaftig figure.

For still others the technology boom has brought forth great opportunity that prior generations of singles didn't have. Robert and Edward can attest to this. There are more online dating sites and more professional matchmakers. Both encourage older folks to meet, mingle, and not go home single. And there's less embarrassment these days about meeting someone those ways.

When Barbara first dated online in 2001, she never shared that fact. She felt a failure in not being able to meet a man in a more traditional way such as attending an event or even perusing the grocery aisles. But these days, it's commonplace, and many who meet online are happy to share that, especially when they go on to happy marriages. About 39 percent of heterosexual couples are reported to have met online, according to a 2017 U.S. study by sociologists Michael Rosenfeld, Reuben Thomas, and Sonia Hausen.[1]

The stats are different for those in the gay community, according to an article, "Surprising Statistics about Gay Dating Online," by Top10. com. Match carries out a survey every year called Singles in America that studies the dating habits of thousands of singles between the ages of 18 and 70. In 2018 while conducting this research, Justin R. Garcia, a PhD at the Kinsey Institute at Indiana University, unearthed some gay online dating stats. He pegs the number of gay couples who meet online at about 70 percent, adding that online dating is on the rise every year whether one is heterosexual or gay, so the stats continue to rise.[2]

To get off on the right footing, we learned through our own dating and others' experiences that it's important to be honest about age rather than backpedal and fess up to the truth later. Sadly, many, whether trans, gay, or straight, initially trim their age. It's also key to be truthful about number of marriages, lifestyle, interests, religion, and anything else important. We've heard and read that too many exaggerate height, finances, and fudge on location and legal status (many don't want to date separated folks, and some don't want to date those who never married or don't have children since they're considered less flexible).

Others use long-ago, glammed-up professional headshots, or photoshop pictures that removed wrinkles, flab, and more. Unfortunately, a look at the heterosexual sites reveals that the number of eligible men dwindles exponentially as we age. The sites seem overloaded with younger female possibilities. Stats back that up since the average life expectancy for a man is now 76.4 years and for women it's 81.2 years, according to data from the Centers for Disease Control and Prevention (CDC).[3]

Exceptions abound and older heterosexual men and women, gay men, and lesbians meet and form loving bonds, sometimes moving in together and marrying. Some prefer to live apart and avoid the financial complications of prenups, and grown children worrying about their inheritances or competition with a partner for their father's or mother's affection and time. However, once again, there's a dearth of eligible older heterosexual and gay men.

The no. 1 reason is that many men, especially heterosexual ones, aren't good at living on their own; they're used to having someone care for them and offer companionship. Although more men may cook thanks to TV shows, food blogs, cookbooks, and classes, these older guys may never have learned how to do so except for basics—boil an egg, open a can of soup, pop a frozen main course in the microwave, pour bottled salad dressing over prewashed lettuce leaves, and grill. To the rescue come the "casserole ladies," a fierce brigade to be reckoned with who know how to reach men's hearts and heads through their growling stomachs, preparing dishes such as Julia Child's coq au vin or *Silver Palate* cookbook's chicken Marbella with prunes—good for aging digestive tracts. This can be true in the gay community as well. The way to many hearts is through their stomachs.

Regardless of sexuality, there are several dating sites to consider. As you peruse them, be sure to have a good attitude and realistic expectations: Silver Singles, a 50-plus-age community, is considered best for single professionals, intelligent matchmaking, and personality testing; Our Time, deemed best for the 50-plus-age dating experience, is known for being a user-friendly site, and doing target matchmaking; Match, the large site that those of many ages and sexual orientations use and one of the original sites, is considered good for expert matchmaking and extensive search filters, and Jdate is for those who are Jewish or want to date Jewish men and women. Margaret tried Our Time for a short time and after three dates; she struck out and left the field.

Some sites charge a membership fee; some offer a free trial. Scrutinize who's online, and read between the lines for red flags, then trust your gut. We learned that if they bash their former or dead wife, as one man did when Margaret met him for coffee, they still may harbor anger and you could indirectly become a target. If they don't have a healthy relationship with grown kids that can be another concern, which Barbara found during several online adventures.

Carefully read about their interests. These matter, we found. If you dislike dogs, don't go for a dog lover; cats, the same, and stay away if they're into boa constrictors (you'd probably rather have a string of pearls around your neck), even if the boa is locked in a cage. If you're not into camping or hiking and you'd rather open a vein than do so, don't expect to start now, which Margaret told one guy she met. Loving those expensive Italian leather hiking boots won't change the experience. Even glamping under a fancy tent can lose appeal if you dislike the great outdoors, except in views through windows, on Instagram, or on picture postcards.

Barbara found that one man's exhaustive search for long-lost relatives in this country and abroad consumed most of their travel time.

WHAT'S IT LIKE TO USE A DATING SITE AND HOW DO YOU CHOOSE THE RIGHT ONE?

So much depends on the profile, photo posted, and timing—who's scrolling through looking at the same time your profile is online. It also depends on the location where you post and sheer numbers of other members since it's almost like throwing darts to see if anything will land in the bull's eye.

Patience, hard work, and humor are required to do a good job in dating online. It can be the equivalent of another job. Most online daters report an initial flurry of interest that may be fun, even intoxicating, and akin to high school rushes as well as sociologically interesting as you encounter men from different walks of life—economically, socially, culturally, racially, intellectually, politically, and geographically. You can limit differences by the filters you choose.

After the ninth, tenth, or twentieth try, so many find that curiosity wears thin as fewer respond. And it's then you may need to push yourself—or have a friend or family member encourage you to rev up interest to continue your search. Barbara found that taking the attitude of you never know kept her going—on 350 dates when she stopped, exhausted, and, yes, discouraged. She had found someone with polar-opposite political views (what was she thinking reading profiles of men in red states when she was all blue?). She was ready to accept not finding anyone for a forever, and then two months later, she was fixed up. Bingo! One widowed male friend of Barbara's, also in his early 70s, has been discouraged about women he's met on dating sites. "My experience," he says, "is that most say the socially proper things about what they are looking for, as do I. I haven't gotten beyond the first date in years," he says.

WHERE ELSE TO MEET NEW FRIENDS AND POTENTIAL DATES—SHIVAS, WAKES, AND FUNERALS

Is it macabre to think that shivas, wakes, and funerals offer an opportunity to socialize in our older years? At first, we thought this was a funny concept. Now, we don't think so. Where else can we go to meet other men—and women—if we give up on Internet dating, have no friends who can fix us up, and everybody we work with is half our age? Rationalize it this way. We know that being socially isolated is bad for our mental and physical health.

These memorial gatherings offer the perfect schmooze-and-connect time with food and drink included for free. If you knew the deceased, a conversation with like-minded and aged friends is great fodder to jumpstart a possible meaningful bond. And then when you're finished talking about poor Aunt Sally, who didn't die as peacefully at home surrounded by loved ones as all those *New York Times* obits intimate that people do, you can move on to current livelier topics—who the caterer is and where your last vacation took you.

Unfortunately, the COVID-19 pandemic of 2020 put a halt to these face-to-face gatherings. However, such startups as *eCondolence.com* and *shiva.com* have introduced "Virtual Gathering." This online tool includes Viewneral™ Platform, virtual get-togethers for wakes, shivas, and other memorial gatherings as another way to honor loved ones and meet potential friends. We say take advantage of all social opportunities, but first master our rules to act your best self.

What to wear if attending in person. Think cocktail or business attire. Women should don one of those sweet little jackets in a dark color that they haven't pulled out of their closets in years, except maybe for Easter or Yom Kippur services. Put a little pin on the lapel like former Secretary of State Madeline Albright does and maybe bring out your strand of pearls, smaller rather than chunkier is more discreet. You can pair your jacket with pants (think Hillary Clinton), a skirt or dress, and wear panty hose like Spanx to hold you in where you bulge. Flats or heels are fine. If you're really old or have bad feet, sneakers are acceptable. A little makeup is okay, but not too much blush. You don't want to look like a twin to the corpse with its large circles of red rouge. And watch the lipstick color. No bright red. Think sweet pink.

How to start a conversation. Since you may not know how sad someone is and their connection to the deceased, be careful. Don't immediately jump into the "Where do you live?" or "Where did you go to college?" stuff. Or, if you're from St. Louis, it's "Where did you go to high school?" Ask how they knew the deceased and for how long. You can proceed to questions about activities you pursued together with the deceased. Don't ask anything too nosey or gossipy such as, "Did you know they had a lot of work done through the years?" We're not talking about work on their home, but their body parts—eyes, noses, breasts, face, and neck lifts. Knee and hip replacements or cataracts are acceptable conversation. Be prudent about funny stories or irreverent statements like saying the deceased looks like a dead ringer for sexy Denzel Washington. Relegate humor to the eulogy since every good one shares one hilarious anecdote.

How to end a conversation. Since you're there to pay your respects and then see and/or meet as many folks as possible to beef up your social life, cut conversations down to no more than 10 minutes and move on. Liken it to speed dating. You can set the alarm on your smartphone to vibrate. Then, blurt out, "That baba ghanoush looks divine. I simply must sample it with some pita or party rye." Who can be offended by such an urge? Speaking of urges, you can also use the best escape question of all, "Where's the bathroom?" Old people understand any bathroom urges.

How to get a phone number or email address to pursue a connection. Since it's tacky to bring out your phone when you're supposed to be sharing sad stories and more; you must think out of the coffin (yes, that box). Plan. Bring along a small stack of business cards with your name, phone number, and email printed on them. You can reach into your purse or pocket, pull one out, and slip it furtively into the person's hand. Say something like, "This has all been so sad, but the one bright spot has been meeting you. Would you like to meet for coffee, wine, or see the latest exhibit at the museum?" Don't push for an answer. If they look shocked, they're not a match.

How to judge the event as a successful social connection. As you stare at the corpse whose life is over or at the closed coffin or urn, remember it's important for you to live life in the present and to the fullest. Weigh how successful you were in mingling and meeting new people at your last shiva call, wake, or funeral. If you get home and find you have made at least one new live contact, you're ahead of the game. If you follow our advice, the possibilities of adding new friends can be infinite, unlike life. Grab the opportunity!

Be realistic about the aging male species. If shopping for a guy, you should beware that many have something that has expired in their packaging. Even if retired or cutting back on work, they may have busy schedules given all the doctor visits and surgeries they may require, as they replace hips, knees, rotator cuffs, or go for cataract surgery even at the younger age of 60. Some older men also require their own bathroom for frequent middle-of-the-night and daytime visits due to an aging prostate, which can mean running for the nearest bathroom and often.

That's not all. Many have unpalatable quirks or annoying habits or let's not forget the mental deterioration that sometimes develops in either sex as age creeps up. Some of our friends now talk about their partner or spouse forgetting more or showing early signs of dementia. We urge friends starting to witness such failures to write down what happens and how often. If the relationship becomes serious, it's important to discuss concerns with the person. Maybe bring concerns up to grown children if they have them and you develop a relationship with them. Suggest they, you, or all of you see appropriate doctors and even an attorney or financial planner to discuss legal and healthcare necessities. However, sometimes, too much neurological damage in a partner may cause the other person to bow out of a relationship if not married. Sounds cruel, but it's something anyone should decide when brutally honest with themself. And beware; the same might happen to you if you're the one who begins to exhibit signs of forgetfulness—and worse.

Women have their issues as well including menopause, bad hips and knees, similar aches and pains, dementia, lung and breast cancers, heart disease, osteoporosis, and diabetes.

While we hate to dampen anybody's enthusiasm, we think it's helpful to offer a peek into what "Priscilla," 72, experienced over the last 12 years. She started to date soon after her first divorce when she was 60 and then a second time at age 69 after her second brief marriage ended. The first time she went on a mad dating rush on a slew of sites—Match, Jdate, OkCupid, Plenty of Fish, and Green Singles; the second time only on Match. Each time she posted her profile, she showed current photos of herself and mentioned her love of travel and certain activities such as yoga, meditation, hiking, and swimming. She also was fixed up a few times.

Initially, she was deluged with emails, probably because of the bigger pool of possibilities. She responded to those who seemed to offer some potential and found after the first few weeks, there was great interest. After she had been on for a month, interest slowed to a trickle. "I then had to do most of the hunting or work." Results were mixed. "I found about 80 percent of those responding to be junky and 20 percent good. It meant a lot of first dates, which I really shouldn't even call a date but a meeting. I decided to give anybody three chances since I knew that people could grow on you. Sometimes you get a bad first impression since they might be nervous or shy." A friend's advice helped. She said rather than go for chemistry go for character, explaining, "Imagine a man putting his arm on you. The test is that you don't gag at the thought of going out with him."

In her years of dating, Priscilla has met about 120 men online. Three proved worth pursuing. Then she was fixed up, and dated a man for 2½ years, even though she saw red flags, including some major idiosyncrasies. She put them aside. She admired his high energy level that matched hers, and he had a great sense of humor. He proposed. Soon after they married, unpleasant behavior surfaced, and after three years they separated. A year later they divorced.

She felt liberated, rewrote her profile, and went back online on Match to search for a long-term guy. "I kept thinking I should go on other sites because my friends were having success on this one or that one. But this time I felt lazier, and it all seemed so much more work." And when she looked at the offerings, she discovered that many of the same men were still there, just older. She also realized that a lot of the good guys came and went quickly. She therefore advises anyone looking regularly and trying to find someone to move fast.

Of late, she's stayed away from sites but focused on a few men who came into her life such as a retired professor and author, whom she eventually lost interest in. "His health wasn't great and there just wasn't chemistry," she says. "He also just seemed very old to me."

Another, "Frank," remains a friend. "He would like to be in a romantic relationship. After dating for a year, I realized there was a disconnect. Example: we went to a concert for our first date and he took me right home. I felt that he couldn't get rid of me fast enough. I threw myself on my bed and cried. But then, he surprised me and asked me out again. He wasn't attractive, even sort of ugly with broad shoulders and I kept waiting for him to kiss me and see what he kissed like. He never did. I couldn't figure out why. Then I dreaded the thought of it when in the beginning I would have welcomed it."

Next came "Stan," a widower who was another fixup rather than an online prospect. It didn't work out in part because of different values. "I like to travel, and he was a homebody. He wouldn't pay for anything. Each paid for what we wanted, including tickets to movies and meals. He also kept talking to me about his late wife and how she was such a terrific cleaner and dresser. I enjoyed hanging out with him, but my gut kept telling me he was not the forever guy."

Yet another widower, "Steve," appeared, who she thought would be the forever-guy, but he also didn't work out. "We met, had an instant attraction, and went to the Pacific Northwest together. It was easy, effortless, and we were together 24/7 for 10 great days. When we were leaving each other at the airport, he found it tough to let go. We wrote love letters, and when together took long walks, kayaked, and had a feeling of joy in each other's company. I had planned a trip to Italy alone, and he told me that I couldn't go without him. He took books out of the library to plan the trip and told me to buy season tickets to one theater for when we came back. There was every indication that this was serious. He showed me his gorgeous ocean-front house in an idyllic vacation spot and introduced me to his grown children. After three months, he went cold and distant on me. We didn't go to Italy together; we stopped going anywhere. Because he was always texting his daughter, I told him I thought they were a bit codependent. 'I don't think you want a woman since you have one and the only thing she doesn't provide is sex!' I said. He said, 'Maybe, you're right.' A week later he called to ask me out for dinner. I texted back 'No,' and wrote a letter describing all that I thought had gone wrong. Maybe he was commitment phobic or maybe it was his daughter. After we called it quits, I saw that he was back online again. It was disappointing. After the COVID-19 pandemic of 2020 hit, I stopped looking for anybody. While I do have a list, I know there is nobody who is going to meet everything on it. Some things are more important than others. You have to decide what you can compromise on and what you can't," she says.

Both of us enjoy companionship and intimacy but we reached different conclusions about dating older men. Part of our feelings stem from how aging has adjusted our romantic priorities. Barbara is thrilled with her relationship with Fixup, as they approach the nine-year mark. He is smart and shares similar political beliefs, which matter to her. He still works as she does, and has many interests, so they're not dependent on each other 24/7. He may lack the peeing-in-your-pants sense of humor that two online dates possessed, but she considers that minor and enjoys laughs from other sources, particularly with Margaret. More important, together Barbara and Fixup share respect, intellectual curiosity, fun, and romance. She says, "We each learned from our prior failed relationships. We communicate well, deal with issues head on, and talk them through rather than run away, get angry, or go silent. We got along fabulously during the pandemic, taking daily walks during warm weather, cooking dinner nightly, and having the advantage of our own homes."

Margaret had a vastly different experience since her husband died ten years ago. After her relationship with someone from her youth ended, she briefly tried online dating, thinking if nothing else it would make great copy. However, she wasn't willing to invest time in an online search. Although she had some fixup opportunities, she wasn't interested in them. She wanted to direct her energy toward moving and building a new life in New York City.

For now, she enjoys living solo. She's often asked, "Are you dating anyone?" Her quick response is "no," without getting defensive or apologetic. She has come to feel she doesn't need a man to complete her with all the projects, classes, and activities she has tried or is interested in pursuing. She's also made new friends. During the pandemic, she says, it would have been nice to have companionship since she rarely left her apartment. Before then, she tried to go out at least one weekend night with a friend or family member but liked to stay in some Friday nights to binge on old movies and catch up on sleep, something that was often interrupted when dating. She's also found it empowering to be able to make all her own decisions rather than make sacrifices as she did as the eldest of four children, a mother of three, wife for 42 years, aunt, and sister-in-law. She takes the attitude that if she meets someone who will allow her to continue her interests, ignore her quirks, accept her family members, and wants her to become part of his, it could be a go . . . maybe.

Even Priscilla says she has mixed emotions about continuing her dating search as she ages. "At times I feel I've learned a lot and at other times I think I've learned nothing," she says. "I know I'm surer of myself and trust my gut feelings more. When you're in a relationship, there's always stuff and the good thing is that it can push your deepest buttons, even if it's trying. When you're not, you go home to your own home alone, and even if you have friends, close ones, and family, there's nobody there to listen to you in the same way. While a friendship is nice, whether with a man or a woman, it doesn't touch your insecurities in the same way that an intimate relationship does. I keep looking at myself, thinking about what I do, accepting my vulnerabilities, and questioning myself. I wonder why I am still single. I remain optimistic, but I also feel when thinking about my dating that I'm like Sisyphus, rolling a rock up this humongous mountain."

There are advantages to looking for love in these older years. We know what we want and may have time for the challenge. However, whether we find a partner as Barbara has or go it alone like Margaret, we realize we have cultivated love in many forms we never expected and know it need not come from one partner. We each have found it with our children, grandkids, other relatives, close friends, work, and hobbies. If it happens to include another person, we have come to accept that it isn't likely to be perfect but may be very good. And by this age, good may be enough.

Chapter Five

If It's Broke, Repair It

Mend and Tend to Relationships Before It's Too Late

At 92, Margaret's mother was in terrible pain. Her mouth hurt so much she could barely eat or talk. Margaret had taken her to three dentists, several oral surgeons, and a mouth cancer oncologist to diagnose the problem. "What if I have cancer?" she asked Margaret one day with fear in her eyes. She did, but it was discovered too late.

She begged Margaret, the eldest of four children and the only one living in her city, "When the time comes, give me a pill. I don't want to live like this." At the time she was one of those old people shuffling glassy-eyed down some nursing home corridor on a walker. This wasn't living; it was existing. The mother Margaret had known—smart, dignified, cultured, and elegant—was slowly disappearing. Because of her refusal to eat, hospice was brought in. She died a day later in what Margaret's family firmly believes was a final act of will.

It was ironic that Margaret had primary responsibility for her mother's care. It was her duty, she felt. But the two clashed at times with vastly different values about money, people, relationships, and politics. However, taking care of her mother became easier because she mellowed as she aged. Although her mother had some dementia, the two were still able to have some nice conversations and mend connections despite having frayed ones in the past. Was it easy listening to her mother complain, sometimes yelling at her, or expressing no gratitude? Absolutely not. This was no time to fight or wage a cold war, Margaret felt.

It's easy to resent having to care for an aging parent, especially when so many may say, "You're so lucky to have them." Yes, we are, but are they so lucky at this age to be alive? So much depends on point of view and circumstances.

The biggest dilemma we face, if we're fortunate still to have our parents, is how much care they need and where they will live as they age. These decisions can be based on what's financially and geographically feasible. Some may move in with us, and if we still have our children at home, this is called multigenerational living, when three generations reside under one roof. Some opt to age in place in their own home, eventually with some outside care. Others may go into an independent living center, or as they decline, step up to assisted living or skilled nursing. As we ponder these decisions for our parents and older relatives, we know we might soon need to confront these decisions for ourselves, as we become the elder generation.

MULTIGENERATIONAL HOUSING

Having multiple generations live together has gained in popularity, but it's an old phenomenon that's new again. Once it was common for several generations to reside together and share incomes and responsibilities. That began to change after World War II with new jobs, increased incomes, and suburbs that began to sprout, spurring a desire for independence. In 1940, about a quarter of the population lived in a multigenerational home; by 1980, just 12 percent did, according to "The Return of the Multi-Generational Family Household" from the Pew Research Center.[1] A range of demographic factors contributed to the decline, namely the rapid growth of nuclear-family suburbs, fewer immigrants, and a rise in the health and economic well-being of adults aged 65 and older.

Due to a host of new factors in recent years, family generations are moving back in together. The prime reasons are a desire to save funds as the economy fluctuates; assist grandparents to age safely as the elderly live longer; help everyone curtail loneliness, recognized as a growing problem for all ages; give boomerang children a place to live before they can be financially independent, and have more hands on deck to watch young or old, do errands, and keep daily life percolating.

"Hispanics (22%), blacks (23%) and Asians (25%) are all significantly more likely than whites (13%) to live in a multi-generational family household," according to Pew Research.[2] To make so much togetherness work well, many experts advocate several caveats. First, adjust surroundings if there are too many steps to the front door, bathrooms without showers, showers without zero-threshold entries, narrow hallways a wheelchair or walker can't move through, stairs to an upstairs level without a chair lift, a low toilet, or high-up storage. Then, there's the emotional adjustment that family members must make to share one home.

Some multigenerational-living experts have learned these lessons firsthand. Lisa Cini, married and with two children, brought her grandmother, who suffered from Alzheimer's disease, and parents into her family's Columbus, Ohio, home to ease her stress. "When elderly parents or grandparents aren't with you, there's nonstop worry, and you sometimes have to drop everything and rush two hours away," she says. What helped Cini prepare was working as a designer in the senior living industry for more than 25 years.

Amy Goyer, an AARP family and caregiving expert, speaker, consultant, and author of *Juggling Life, Work and Caregiving*, also brought her aging parents into her Phoenix home. After her mother died, her father remained through the course of his Alzheimer's disease, and her sister and two nephews moved in with them for a year before moving to the house next door.

Both women knew from their work that two essentials must be present to make living together work well over a long term. Each family member requires some privacy. In ideal scenarios, often not available, that means a private bedroom and bathroom that's been remodeled or already functions well for someone older, a living area, and access to the outdoors, or an apartment with a door to a hallway and another door to the outdoors for freedom of access.

More home builders are taking the needs of the aging population into consideration by constructing new homes with apartments within houses or condos or at least setting aside a room or suite on a ground-floor level. Kolter Homes LLC, a developer and homebuilder headquartered in Palm Beach Gardens, Florida, is continuing to incorporate multigenerational living quarters within its homes. To date, those built in North and South Carolina and Georgia are located in a daylight basement space, giving the multiple generational members their own private quarters. In Florida, where there are no basements, they may be built above a garage or in a separate casita, either attached or detached. One prototype house that sold has a one-level walkout basement with an in-law suite that contains an open family room with kitchenette, master suite, guest suite, patio, optional media room, and elevator to the first level.

Existing homes can also be retrofitted to work for seniors by widening doorways and halls for wheelchairs and walkers; lowering or raising bathroom and kitchen sinks to be better able to reach a faucet or use from a wheelchair; investing in a higher toilet; lowering countertops and high-up storage; replacing a traditional tub with a walk-in model; adding a kitchenette with microwave, sink, and small refrigerator if there's no full second kitchen to give a greater feeling of independence; changing out lamps with stronger bulbs as eyesight fails; and rearranging a laundry area so machines aren't stacked and too high to reach. If possible when there's an outdoor space, plant more low-maintenance materials that require less water, install a sprinkler system if in the budget, and plant flowers and shrubs in raised planters to avoid bending.

The second essential is having a written or verbal plan that all family members try to live by. It's the equivalent of what many family members in business together follow to divide tasks and get along. Part of the agreement should include having a good attitude yet knowing there will be periodic ups and downs, being patient when mishaps occur, communicating immediately when things go awry rather than letting frustrations spiral out of control, and having a strategy in place to resolve disagreements. Some families find that it's wise to schedule meetings to talk over differences. Differences often center around planning mealtimes and consuming meals since preferences for food and time to eat may vary. Cini and Goyer each discovered food to be a major disrupter. Cini also found unexpected visits from extended family and her kids' friends necessitated rules in advance.

SILVER LININGS

Many families who undertake multigenerational living discover numerous plusses, from knowing their family members better to gaining a better understanding of family history and teaching younger members about the life cycle and patience required to adjust to each age group. Cini learned her grandmother was more than a homemaker. "Not that there's anything wrong with that, but it did make it difficult for me to connect with her. She was the grandmother who did all the cooking and canning, all the cleaning, went to church, always looked perfect, never drove a car, and combed my grandfather's hair every day.

"When you see relatives on holidays it's typically pleasant but superficial. 'How are you feeling?' 'What have you been up too?' 'Oh, that's nice,' and then it's over and you are back to your home and they are back to theirs. However, when you live together, you connect on a much deeper level. I found out that my grandmother, born in 1922, was on the girls' basketball team, played the violin, and was the lead in the high school musical! It was such a mindset shift for me. I felt more comfortable sharing with her my challenges and dreams. She loved going to the kids' soccer games. I thought it was because she loved them (which was true), but she was also an athlete and competitive. Had we not lived together, I would never have understood who she really was and how I was a lot like her in more ways than I thought."

Other family members also reaped benefits. When Cini asked her son, Jacob, 17, what his silver lining was he sent back a heartfelt note, titled, "Silver Linings of Multigenerational Living." Among its nuggets were, "Multigenerational living allowed me to do something that very few others will ever do. It allowed me to see through the eyes of a woman that experienced every change in the modern era. Gaining an understanding and respect for lives that have been lived before me [has] enabled me to be in the position that I am today. By that I mean, great grandma gave me the ability to connect and empathize with anyone of any age because that is what I saw her do daily."

AGING IN PLACE AND OTHER OPTIONS

If multigenerational living isn't an option, perhaps having your parent or loved one age in place in their own home might be. That's the first choice of most elder adults at the later stage of the life curve.

If a family member ages at home, your job might become that of unpaid primary caregiver and supervisor of daily tasks—grocery shopper, medical middle person, cook, bather, repair person, social connector, spiritual consult, and more. Marti Stricker, who lives in St. Louis,

Missouri, took on the role of primary caregiver to her aging mom. The intent was to have her mother age in place with Stricker in charge, but dementia and other health issues forced her finally to put her mother into assisted living for almost 3½ years. Stricker still oversaw her care, but the burden was lessened. Because Stricker has no children, she has given a great deal of thought to whom she can count on if her husband were to predecease her, to oversee her daily care and finances. She hopes to age in place. "Right now, we really don't have a particular person who would be able to do that daily.

"Possibly a nephew or 'niece,' who really isn't a niece but daughter to my husband's cousin. On a short-term basis, I am hoping they would be able to help out," Stricker says. She also is toying with the idea of doing something an aunt did. She found an independent person to help manage her daily living—drive her, accompany her to doctor's appointments, and make sure bills got paid.

Whether an immediate family member or a more distant relative is willing to take on the responsibility, the demands on any caregiver may lead to several challenges. If you're the designated person, that could mean disruption of your schedule like it was disrupted for Stricker. The result may range from mildly upsetting to infuriating.

It's tough not to let anger build, which, in turn, might lead to depression when calls come day and night that your loved one isn't taking their meds, or has shouting obscenities, fallen, or in worst cases needs an operation. Most likely you're at a time in your life when you hoped to kick back but instead find your time consumed by caregiving duties. And if your elderly parent doesn't have adequate funds to pay and no long-term insurance, you may have to dip into your savings, as a New York friend of Margaret's revealed she's had to do for her 97-year-old father. He lives in an independent living facility and ran out of money.

Barbara's mother aged in place for 25 years in her New York City apartment until she died at almost 101 years old. Before she died, aides came in for longer periods as she lost most of her ability to maintain her daily life functions. Barbara would have preferred to bring her into her home, but her two-story house didn't afford a proper layout and couldn't be remodeled to work. Also, moving her mother at such a late stage—or even when younger—to a facility might have resulted in heartbreaking consequences, even depression, since she would be separated from favorite views, possessions, and routines.

To age in place in later years usually requires hiring a competent caregiver from a few hours a day or week to full-time paid care unless there's a family member willing to step up to the plate. Many family members do so because the cost of outside caregiving can come close to $250,000 for a full-time aide vetted by an agency in a metropolitan area like New York City. If the aide gets sick or takes a better job, what happens? Some families find it best to hire two people to split the hours and demands of cooking, cleaning, bathing, and talking to their charge.

The need for cost-effective solutions that help people age independently with safety and comfort in our homes gave rise to the development of the Naturally Occurring Retirement Community Supportive Services Program (NORC-SSP) model in 1986.

A NORC is a neighborhood, subdivision, building, or geographic area that was not originally designed for older people, but now has a large percentage of residents over age 60. NORCs can be "vertical" (e.g., high-rise buildings in New York City) or "horizontal" (e.g., suburban neighborhoods with a combination of single-family homes, condos, and apartments). Coordinated by local nonprofits or government agencies, the NORC-SSP unites health and social-service providers and housing entities, aids older community members in identifying needs, and offers programs and services that support independent living. For a modest annual membership fee, many NORC-SSPs provide a variety of social programs and classes and use volunteers to fix appliances, change lightbulbs, and troubleshoot issues with technology. NORC-SSPs are largely funded through local governmental grants.

Sarah Levinson, manager of the successful St. Louis NORC that started in 2002, says that their current membership includes nearly 700 people ranging in age from 60 to 103. "With changes to the aging landscape—people living and staying healthy longer combined with an increasing number of organizations offering programs and services geared toward supporting the ever-growing aging population—NORC-SSPs are evolving and adapting to meet the needs of community members," Levinson says.

More recently, the Village to Village Network, a nonprofit association of villages, was incorporated in 2010. However, the first village to form in this movement was in Boston's Beacon Hill in 2001. The concept was started by residents who wanted to connect with their neighbors, and its focus is social connection with a neighbor-to-neighbor model. A set of guidelines on its website, https://www.vtvnetwork.

org, is used to form a Village. Says Pazit Aviv, village coordinator of Montgomery County, Maryland, "This movement is a recognition that we have not as a society given enough value to new relationship building. This is an attempt to recreate the social aspects of our communities of the past with cohesive neighborhoods and neighbors that offered reciprocity and mutual care."

Some villages have paid staff in addition to volunteers and charge a membership fee. Others are composed of all volunteers and charge no fee. Community members run the show. They offer transportation to medical appointments, the grocery store, and other places, help with simple tasks at home, and offer (nonmedical) assistance for someone just out of a hospital. Villages may organize events and outings that can take place at a neighbor's home or at a local church, synagogue, mosque, library, or community recreation center. During the coronavirus of 2020, villages were uniquely positioned to help residents stay connected, says Barbara Sullivan, executive director of the Village to Village Network movement, which currently has 380 known villages throughout the world and estimates it reaches some 40,000 seniors.

In a growing number of markets, there's similar help from young college-age, vetted students through Papa Inc., a digital health company based in Miami that describes itself as "Family on Demand," and links the elderly who are still home through an on-demand app. Among the duties they take on are transportation, house chores, technology, meals, and companionship. To date, the company is in all 50 states.

Some of the larger insurance companies are also stepping up to offer services to keep the aging in place. Chubb North America offers a personal risk service in which an agent goes into an insured member's home and recommends resources that a homeowner can tap into to stay safe. Aetna Medicare offers a program to help members and caregivers access and supplement benefits through such services as meal deliveries or transportation to appointments. There are home auditors surfacing to help clients analyze which changes to make.

HOW TO HIRE A CAREGIVER

If the preferred route is to find a skilled, caring person so an elderly person can age in their home or in a relative's, that usually takes time and patience due to a surge in the aging population and a decrease in competent help. Approximately 41 million unpaid family caregivers provided an estimated 34 billion hours of care—worth a staggering $470 billion—to their parents, spouses, partners, and friends in 2017, according to the AARP's series, "Valuing the Invaluable."[3] Family caregivers now encompass more than one in five Americans, according to the 2020 update to another AARP and National Alliance for Caregivers (NAC) report, *Caregiving in the U.S. 2020.* From 2015 to 2020, the number of family caregivers increased by 9.5 million people, going from 43.5 million to 53 million.[4]

These numbers are expected to climb, though the big question mark is how life after the 2020 coronavirus pandemic might alter them and how we can care for one another in the future, says Grace Whiting, president and CEO of Washington, DC-based NAC. In general, she expects people to be more squeezed, namely because family size is diminishing so there are fewer offspring to share the burden, medical technology is helping the elderly to live longer, and there's a lot of pressure on the younger generations, she says. Some of that pressure extends beyond their caring for older generations. "They have been more saddled with student loans and debt and aren't as successful as their parents and grandparents were. At the same time, they want to find time to enjoy their lives, which creates another pressure point," she says.

All these stressors take a toll. The study revealed that family caregivers were in worse health compared to five years ago. That may not be fully accurate given the long-term effect of the damage from the coronavirus in 2020. For many, their caregiving role has lasted an average of 4½ years, and in some cases the damage has been physical and in other cases emotional due to feelings of guilt and isolation.

Yet, whether these family caregivers took on their role because there was nobody else or it represented a cultural tradition, many find joy in doing so. What often helps is having access to some type of care for themselves, which might include being part of a support group or tapping into solutions through Facebook groups online; having society and others value the role they play; understanding there's no straight trajectory on how old age will unfold—physically and mentally and certainly with new illnesses such as the coronavirus, so they can be prepared rather than surprised—and holding on to the beliefs they and their family value most. Conversation throughout the journey is important to avoid making quick decisions in a crisis, Whiting says. "Families should talk early on and make decisions about care long before needed."

And even when you think you've found a good caregiver, you might be in for a rude awakening. Some may leave to take a better-paying job. Some don't work out due to "elder abuse" that may be physical, emotional, or financial. Betsy Gold, cofounder of LeanOnWe, which helps families hire private, independent home aides in Metro New York, New Jersey, and Connecticut, says that caregiver financial abuse accounts for $6.67 billion in annual losses, which is why it's essential to take the time to perform extensive background and reference checks.

Abuse is not always due to an outside caregiver but can happen with a grown child or family friend. The person starts by borrowing money or removing valuable items from the home. It also may happen with the senior's lawyer or financial planner who takes advantage of an aging client. Gold suggests regularly reviewing financial statements to check on their accuracy, removing important financial and legal documents from the home, and putting valuables in a safe deposit box, storage unit, or other secure location. If abuse of any kind is suspected, there are resources you may contact such as the National Center on Elder Abuse.

Even though Barbara lived two hours from her mother's apartment, she initially became the main caregiver because she felt she had the time and ability to help. Also, she had promised her late father she would do so. However, after taking on the responsibilities, she recognized the need for backup from part-time help due to her work and distance. It was far from easy to find someone to come in once or twice a week and help bathe and feed her mother and run errands. She looked on a bulletin board in her mother's building where names are posted, found an available aide, and vetted her through references. She increased the timetable after her mother fell and returned home from a rehabilitation facility.

Others can follow the advice of coauthors Amanda Lambert and Leslie Eckford, who suggest in their book, *Aging with Care: Your Guide to Hiring and Managing Caregivers at Home*, that going online and searching for the word "home health care" or calling a licensed elder-care agency such as LeanOnWe or Mavencare is wise. If the caregiver match isn't good, many agencies permit a switch, even multiple switches. If a caregiver fails to show up, the agency will find a replacement. Barbara hired Mavencare aides after her mother had a mild stroke five years ago. While some aides appealed to her mother more than others, they all offered quality care.

When meeting with the potential candidate, consider asking:

1. How long have you worked as a caregiver?
2. Please provide two to three references.
3. May I see your passport, driver's license, or other proof of citizenship?
4. Are you willing to accept payment by check, PayPal, Venmo, or a similar service?
5. Let's discuss hours. What are you looking for? Here's what I'm thinking.
6. How much do you expect to be paid hourly?
7. What tasks will you handle—bathing, feeding, reading, talking, playing music, taking outdoors for a walk (if possible) or sitting outdoors, fielding phone calls, cooking, going to doctor appointments or to church, and walking a dog?
8. What cleaning tasks in the house will you handle? Is there anything you aren't willing to do?
9. Are you able to lift the patient out of the bathtub, on to a bed, or off the toilet if they need the help?
10. Do you understand that the patient may become verbally abusive at times, which is not intended to be personal? Can you handle that? We will ask the doctor for help with medications, if needed.
11. How can we best communicate? By text, email, cell phone? How often should we talk—maybe in the morning or evening daily?
12. Do you have a backup to offer in case you get sick or need time with family? If so, we should meet that person, too.
13. Do you understand not to come to work if you're sick?
14. Can you handle calls with workmen if something needs repair?

When Barbara knew she couldn't be at her mom's apartment enough and her family detected the physical and emotional tolls the job was taking on Barbara, she found two women to divide the workload. Both were certified, experienced health aides. Neither was the adult version of a Mary Poppins, but both seemed more than "good enough" and showed up on time. One of the two eventually "vanished." Fortunately, the other aide filled in with a promise that a sister or friend would help if she felt she found the job demanding.

HOW TO PREPARE A HOME FOR AGING IN PLACE

There's a growing body of resources to get started that are worth perusing. Many organizations initially evaluate the patient and home—seeing that area rugs are rolled up, that there's sufficient light, ample means to cook and store food, comfortable places to sit and lie down, safe bathrooms, raised toilet seats, cleaning supplies, and aging aids such as a walker, wheelchair, handheld shower faucet, a grabber, and grab bars. Some organizations charge a fee for this service.

After a terrible accident while bicycling caused Rosemarie Rossetti, PhD, to become paralyzed and unable to live comfortably in her and husband Mark's home, the couple decided to construct a Universal Design Living Laboratory home in Columbus, Ohio (www.udll.com). The goal was to showcase what is needed to live independently at any age and especially for those older people who want to stay put and age in place.

The couple had their new home constructed from scratch to include a range of features that offer safety, independence, and accessibility. For example, every entrance is step free and 36 inches wide. The floor space is open around the island and appliances. The counter tops and shower are wheelchair accessible. An elevator was installed that goes from the lower level to a loft.

Since her accident, Rossetti has become an internationally known speaker with her business, Rossetti Enterprises Inc., as well as a consultant, writer, and publisher about the topic. She has written several important books that offer good resources for anybody embarking on this journey for themselves or a loved one.

Architect Jeffrey DeMure, AIA, offers suggestions in his book, *Livable Design,* such as putting essential spaces on a main level including a first-floor bedroom, zero-step entry, and good circulation flow within to move about and kitchens and bathrooms that accommodate the elderly. Some of the changes may not cost more than "regular" features but some will add up. A chair lift may run about $2,000, but an elevator can cost as much as $15,000 between two levels and more for additional floors. The home or condominium also requires a large closet-sized space to accommodate it.

There's more good news about the growing arsenal of tools to help, which Cini lists in her book *BOOM: The Baby Boomers Guide to Leveraging Technology.* Technology is at the forefront with robots that vacuum, mow a lawn, and even help cook. What's essential is a high-speed Internet connection. Cini is in the process of renovating a 1914 house that will be outfitted with the latest tech for multigenerational living and aging in place.

WITNESSING DECLINE UP CLOSE

Barbara found it difficult watching her once energetic mother deteriorate. After her 96th birthday, her good health waned when she had a small stroke, which required speech and physical therapy. Barbara took on more chores and would race around to shop and cook her mother's favorite foods or whatever she'd eat as she became pickier. She also bought supplies and took out large print books from the library. She helped with her mother's financial choices, made doctor and dentist appointments, and escorted her mother to them before she became less mobile. She also checked with the pharmacist about medicines and vaccinations.

She found herself mustering Herculean patience as her mother repeated herself or insisted she couldn't hear and forgot what she had said. Her filter worsened, and she began hurling insults, one time telling Barbara in front of a bank teller, "Have you talked to your physician about your weight gain?" Barbara cut her off, saying, "In front of a stranger is not the time. I'm dealing with it." At other times, her mother reverted to two-year-old behavior as her cognitive skills started to decline. "If I eat two bites of my meatloaf, may I have a cookie?"

After a fall that required being in a rehabilitation facility for six weeks, she showed further decline and was less interested in living. Once home, she seemed to rally initially, and Barbara hired more help to alleviate her burden. Barbara's mother began to have a harder time navigating with her walker.

Food became a greater battleground. She complained about the food Barbara prepared and which she once loved. She often told Barbara, like a bad Yelp reviewer, "I hate the quiche," or "That macaroni and cheese is awful. I want a real meal." Barbara began to feel she was running a restaurant with an always disgruntled guest.

Then Barbara began to lose her much-needed sleep. Her mother started to awaken in the middle of the night because she was hungry.

She would clunk with her walker down the hall to the table and angrily demand food. Mostly, her mother craved sugar—in maple syrup, red Jell-O, cookies, cakes, and lactose-free ice cream, day or night. Barbara worried whether so much sugar hurt her mother since she had stopped brushing her teeth and lost a few. Barbara would awaken with the noise and explain that it was the middle of the night, and there was no food until morning.

Her mother began to insult the aides and physical therapist coming to help her. A typical conversation with a sweet young physical therapist went like this, "You're so lucky you're married since you're not pretty." Barbara would ask her mother to apologize and bring her back to reality. Her mom was shocked at her own words. Yet, she went on to regularly insult one caregiver with, "You have the biggest behind," and the other with words too hurtful to share. Barbara knew it wasn't her mom speaking but her evil twin who had entered her aging brain like some alien. A physician prescribed medicine to soften her tone and improve her sleep.

Barbara kept trying to right the ship, which she equated with an elegant sinking cruise liner. As her mother's condition worsened, she tried a host of activities to enrich her mother's life, including reading books to her out loud and showing photos of her granddaughters and great-grandchildren on her phone. Barbara encouraged loyal friends and family to visit. She brought in a hairdresser to cut and wash her Mom's thinning white hair. She purchased a medical alert device to warn of falls and a baby monitor to use in a second bedroom so anyone staying over could hear her. She switched to a medical service at a nearby hospital that made house calls.

For Barbara, a tough part was learning to balance her needs versus her mother's wishes in the stereotypical reversal of roles. With the advice of a family therapist, Barbara scaled back her time with her mother to conserve her energy and sanity. "I may go crazy if I keep at this," she confided to Margaret. As her mother continued to decline, she remained sharp enough to tell Barbara she wanted to talk about her funeral, a request Barbara resisted, then agreed to. They discussed the graveside service she wanted. Barbara shared that she had asked a family friend who is a rabbi to officiate. And she began writing a eulogy in her head.

FACING BURNOUT: WHY DO THIS?

Legions of women, younger, including many millennials, or older, are caregivers for aging parents and other relatives who have made it into their 90s, even advanced 90s, and centenarian years. Barbara would joke periodically about her mother, "She'll probably outlive me." Most centenarians, like Barbara's mom, live on borrowed time with less memory, more physical ailments, a fear of falling, and lack of motivation (or energy) to care about good hygiene and appearance. These factors make taking on the burden of caregiver or manager of caregivers huge and stressful.

As difficult as the emotional and physical load was, Barbara tried to focus on the good times together but also got away when she could. On a weekend escape with a childhood friend, she consulted a clairvoyant who told her after studying her cards that this period would not last forever. As Margaret said jokingly afterward when told of the conversation, "You needed to pay for this advice? I could have told you the same."

A COACH'S WISE COUNSEL

Ken Druck, PhD, an expert in family psychology, stresses the importance of getting to the root of why we're doing the caregiving in his best-selling book, *Raising an Aging Parent: Guidelines for Families in the Second Half of Life*. In several email exchanges, he suggested that we and others ask ourselves: "Am I doing this because it's expected in our family for the daughter, the eldest, or the one who lives closest to the aging person to do so?" "Because I expect a big payback?" "Because it's expected of me, to show my parents I'm their most loyal and loving child?" "Because I'm a type-E person, the one to be everything to everybody (except to ourselves for whatever reason)?" Getting clear about why we're making the sacrifices and investing the time and energy necessary for effective caregiving, he advises, can help us make midcourse corrections and rededicate ourselves to taking care of our mother or father.

Although Barbara's reasons were altruistic, she still bristled when her mother made frequent demands, "Where is my food?" or "What's taking so long?" Barbara thought, "How can I continue to handle this?"

REMEMBERING THE AXIOM
ABOUT SELF-CARE FOR THE CAREGIVER

A chapter in Druck's book, "How Much Is Enough: The Real Responsibilities of Adult Children," resonated for each of us. We've come to realize that caring for our parents as they age can reawaken jealousies, grudges, and resentments that exist in most all families. Druck advises us to do what we can to de-escalate and opt out of family drama and dysfunction—and to reward ourselves with self-care on a regular basis, taking stress breaks, exercising, and doing whatever is necessary to refill our cups. By balancing the care we're giving an aging parent with the care we're giving ourselves, we promote good health and prevent burnout.

As we look at the big picture, regardless of prior and present animosity, we realize we've all had good times with our parents. It's important to bear in mind that we share so much—DNA, history, family, love, and typically a lot of angst after both generations have lived so long. For Barbara, before her mother's big decline, there were many bright spots. On certain days, her mother reverted to her younger self—who put others first, shared her joy of baking, museums, and travel, complimented Barbara on a recipe she prepared, or an article or artwork that she shared. Occasionally, Barbara patted herself on the back when she was able to engage her mother in a normal, if even brief, conversation.

Establish a routine. A big part of smart caregiving that will help a caregiver stay sane is to establish a routine, so you feel a modicum of control.

Here are other ideas:

Make a list of what needs to be done daily, from cooking to cleaning, safety, hygiene, and medications. If it helps, write on a whiteboard, or make a poster with the list, put it in a place that's visible, and look at it daily, or do an Excel spreadsheet.

Find what you are willing to take on and farm out the rest.

Try to be present when you can, another way to ward off the elderly person's loneliness. That means putting aside your phone or computer to have an eyeball-to-eyeball conversation.

Find what gives pleasure, whether large-print books, books on tape, old movies, looking at photo albums or photos on your iPad, sharing past vacations and trips, or asking the elderly person to talk about the past.

If you don't want to cook for the aging parent or spouse, try a food delivery service. Many cities offer a free one for the elderly. Barbara's mother didn't like the one they tried; she wanted Barbara's cooking.

Check into smart technology for seniors and sign up for a medical protective device. These are worn around the neck, so you don't have to stand at the elderly person's side 24/7 to avoid falls. Make sure it's waterproof. These come in all sorts of variations—some require an upfront payment, others just a monthly charge; still others require a commitment of three or maybe six months. Some alert a local emergency room and others a family member; some go off if the person falls or only if the person calls a special number or presses a button. It's best to go online, read, and compare types and prices.

Essentials to have on hand before the journey begins. In her well-researched, thorough book *The Conscious Caregiver*, Linda Abbit, a family caregiver and founder of Tender Loving Eldercare, a blog and online community, asks and answers some of the most key questions for the caregiver-recipient relationship to succeed.

Ideally, you will discuss before a crisis hits such issues as medical treatments, end-of-life ceremonies, legal documents that need to be up to date, dispersal of possessions, and more. Make sure all essential documents are in order, signed, and kept safely in the cloud, printed, and stored in a safe deposit vault, or on a disk or external hard drive. You want them ready when you need access. Have everything shored up to avoid legal and family tangles and last-minute scrambling for names, phone numbers, and passwords. Have these easily accessible:

Your parent's or spouse/partner's Social Security number. Many insurers require this information, plus phone number, address, and birth date.

A credit card. You need this or a checking account to order groceries and pay help, and to buy medical devices such as a blood pressure measuring cup, bed rail, and medications.

Medicaid or Medicare cards, supplemental Medicare health insurance card, and drug plan card. You need these when accompanying your friend or family member to a doctor or hospital.

Copy of a long-term insurance plan or life insurance plan with a long-term care rider. If the person has purchased this insurance, have a copy and know when it kicks in and other details.

Names, phone numbers, and email addresses of their lawyer, accountant, physicians, bank (and contact person there), and financial planner. Alert them if there are health changes and be sure you are on all the documents needed, which may require a signature and even having a notary to sign it and watch you sign it. Other witnesses might be required as well. If not, you may not have access to information you require. Make sure you've signed papers with the bank to get into their safe deposit boxes. Again, it's best if you check in advance with the right professionals and periodically update documents and signatures according to state rules.

Chain of command. In an emergency, Margaret's mother's chain of command was to call her primary care physician. Next Margaret was to be called since she had power of attorney for her mother's healthcare. Then, her wish was to be taken to urgent care if the matter wasn't too serious or to call 911 and take her to the emergency room (with the list of preferred hospitals to be shared with the EMI care team).

If you're the health care proxy, make sure you have the papers available if there's an emergency.

Here are a few other documents you will want to make sure you have signed, notarized and close at hand, if required. Andrew M. Mitchell, a St. Louis, Missouri, trust and estates attorney with Kirkland Woods & Martinsen LLP, explains what they are.

Durable power of attorney. This document allows you to make financial decisions with someone else's money.

Health care power of attorney. This document allows you to name someone to make health care decisions for you when you cannot make them yourself.

Living will and will. The living will expresses the elderly person's wishes when they face a terminal situation since they may not be able to communicate and state, "Please, do not resuscitate (called a DNR) or intubate." There is also the will. Every will does say who gets the property of the maker of the will, but some just give property outright, not in trust. It covers who gets what, when, and how. "You really wanted the silver? Sorry, if Mom made a list and deemed it was going to Junior; you got her portrait. Congrats!"

If you have a trust, you might want a pour-over will as well to avoid probate. However, a pour-over will does not avoid probate by itself. Property that has to pass according to a pour-over will into a previously established revocable trust does so through probate. The way to avoid probate with a revocable trust is to title the assets in the name of the trust before death, Mitchell explains.

Trust(s). There are revocable and irrevocable trusts, says Mitchell. A revocable trust is a beneficiary part of a well-crafted estate plan as it helps to avoid probate and can also serve as a vehicle for management of the creator's assets in the event of his or her incapacity during their lifetime. However, a revocable trust does not have any advantages in saving estate taxes over a will; it just avoids probate, so it is the most common primary estate planning document for most people, who do not have estate tax concerns.

An irrevocable trust, says Mitchell, can also be created by a will. In that case, it would be called a testamentary trust. An irrevocable trust enables someone else to make decisions for a beneficiary after the death of the benefactor. Perhaps a grandchild receives an inheritance of $100,000 but the person who died—the grandmother—had determined and stated in the trust that only $10,000 was to be given each year to protect the assets from being depleted foolishly in one fell swoop. Often, they are created under revocable trust agreements—as a sub trust becoming effective only upon the death of the person creating the revocable trust.

Caregiving for Barbara ebbed and flowed. During the coronavirus pandemic of 2020, it became more stressful since she had to stop visiting her mother often for safety reasons. She managed food and medical supplies by phone and online, reported to the doctor changes and a need for new medicines, checked with the aide twice daily, and tried to talk to her mom every day. She knew her mother would not get better, but there were days when her mother was more lucid, engaged, and happier.

Barbara became more convinced about her decision to keep her mother at home since many nursing homes reported increased cases of death from the coronavirus. Barbara was able to be with her before she died. She held her hand and spoke to her, and took Margaret's advice that she put her own cell phone up to her mother's ear so her granddaughters and great-grandsons could whisper their final goodbyes.

The positive connection Margaret felt after caring for her mother was palpable. Margaret remembers hospice telling her that the last sense to go is hearing. So, leaning down when her mother was dying with their cheeks pressed together, she whispered into her mother's ear that it was fine to let go. This granted Margaret a tender farewell—and her mother a final measure of grace.

Chapter Six

Ills, Pills, and Spills

Sharing and Caring in Proper Doses

We consider ourselves nurturers. Under normal circumstances, we call friends and ask how they are and what we can do for them, or just listen, even if the news is about their hemorrhoids, root canals, colonoscopies, and mammograms. Because we care, we also check in regularly with elderly relatives and our grown kids. And we brief each other daily, almost in presidential "BREAKING NEWS" style, about what's good, bad, or funny in our lives and health.

As reporters, we've been trained to gather and share information. We've mastered how to dispense big doses of sympathy and empathy, along with understanding the difference. Sympathy is feeling compassion, sorrow, or pity for hardships another person encounters. Empathy is putting ourselves in that person's shoes. One advantage of getting older is wisdom gained from experience. Our perspective at 50, 60, 70, or 80 is different than that of our 20- and 30-year-old selves.

Here are examples. We might find a certain exercise, type of meditation, or medication that works well for whatever is going on in our bodies and emotional lives. We embrace it and then dole out our advice to those we think might be interested. We try to pick up on clues if there's interest—a head nodding "yes" or questions, or a head shaking "no" or dead silence. In the latter case, we try to stop from pushing. Many can ingest only a certain amount, and don't want to overdose on information from too many sources.

Our friends tend to do the same and share advice and caring. We balance our gratitude with what we can absorb, which also might depend on our mood and the delivery. When Barbara broke two bones in her right hand, she was inundated with advice, some helpful, especially from a medical doctor/friend who said, "You'll probably be okay going to a doctor in your area, but I don't deal in probably. Go see the expert at my hospital in New York City who's a trauma expert and does this work all the time." She did and had a good result, not perfect, but possibly as good as it could be given the extent of the breaks and her age.

There were also times when Barbara didn't want advice, just an ear. A casual friend told her how she should deal with her physical therapy and whom she should consult. She then threw into the mix how Barbara needed to hire more help for her aging mother. Her advice probably was sound, but her tone was bossy and she gave too much information. The friend also hadn't first asked if Barbara wanted advice—just jumped in and pummeled her in ra-ta-tat style.

When Margaret was dealing with her late husband's five-year illness, along came a nonstop litany of questions from well-meaning friends. She was surprised and overwhelmed. During this period of unprecedented stress and fatigue, Margaret often fielded directives and queries. Two particularly galling ones asked by several well-meaning friends and work colleagues after her husband was diagnosed were, "Did you get a second opinion?" and "How are you doing?" Duh!

If we or a loved one have an issue, each of us tries to find the best resources to try to fix it. Not everything can be fixed, but we talk about it because that's how we process. And at times, overprocess. We call these discussions about illness "organ recitals," whether sleep apnea, cataracts, polyps, worn knees, chronic illnesses, or various cancers. The remedies typically involve sleep machines, cholesterol meds, laparoscopic surgeries for worn parts, and lap bands and gastric bypasses for pounds that can't be shed from every diet tried—Scarsdale, Atkins, Paleo, Cabbage Soup, and Keto. Humor is critical as is reserving energy to share woes for those closest to us.

The problem is that the devil is in the details as many, sometimes including ourselves, share specifics of every medical appointment, test result, diagnosis, treatment, prognosis, and doctor and hospital visited. In some cases, being fixated on our health and others' leads us to check out numerous online medical sites and journals, many of which spew false information. Oftentimes, we come up with armchair diagnoses for ourselves and friends. Doing so may do more harm by raising greater, sometimes unfounded concerns, rather than creating a sense of calm. When Margaret's husband was diagnosed with cancer, his oncologist urged him not to read advice on websites. He cheated occasionally. She didn't and preferred to ask the doctors questions in an email or in person.

However, if truth be told, who wants to hear everything about everyone's aches, pains, and illnesses? It's not that we don't care. But enough is enough. Who needs a diatribe on the wisdom of opting for generic drugs or going for pricier brands? Let's also not forget the side effects that almost every drug presents as a possibility to launch into another long-winded discussion. (Phew, we're out of breath already.) In our new, improved sharing economy, we can overshare. How unpalatable it is to discuss details of a colonoscopy at lunch while crunching a Cobb salad (with a low-calorie dressing, which might lead to a different line of food-obsessed conversations). We're compassionate when someone presents with a serious illness or has a family member with one. But we strive to maintain balance much like we try to do most of the time in our eating habits.

HEALTHY PRESCRIPTIONS FOR
HOW TO REACT TO LESS SERIOUS MALADIES

Over time, we developed what we consider a healthy prescription for endless exchanges about less serious maladies connected with aging such as bunion surgery and removal of noncancerous moles. These are the chats that make eyes roll and cause people to nod off when listening to banter about 50 shades of surgery, the best pills to take for urinary incontinence, or a discourse on the merits of the new women's or men's Viagra.

We have a friend of a family member who blindsided us when she shared in detail about a most private body part, her vagina, which was causing her pain. We listened, and learned more about her vagina than we probably know about ours or anybody else's. We gently attempted to shift the conversation to back pain. We tried to be sympathetic and empathetic.

In typical fashion when someone isn't feeling well, we like to bring them a treat to make them feel better. What, we wondered, is the proper gift to send a person when her vagina isn't in working order? Chicken soup is for colds, tea is for sore throats, Gatorade is for dehydration, but what the hell do you send someone to help ease a painful vagina? We came up with a few:

- an ice pack to numb the area,
- Epsom salts and suggest a soak in a tub,
- comfortable 100 percent cotton underwear that has the days of the week embroidered on them so she can keep track of the "good" days, and
- a book on how to do Kegel exercises.

We decided that it is better to try to avoid initiating or participating in certain medical discussions by following our healthy-minded suggestions the next time we ask, "How are you? Are you okay?" Like ripping off a Band-Aid®, end a conversation swiftly and let fresh air (and other topics) into the room. This can be just what a doctor might order.

Find upbeat subjects to discuss. Once the discussion turns to certain body functions that cause your eyebrows to rise higher than the East/West Gateway Arch in St. Louis (our shared city) it's time to shift gears. Said one friend, "It's good to share certain information with friends like creams and lotions. But when the conversation is about bowel issues that becomes too graphic, I deflect and start talking real fast about the latest book I'm reading." Some neutral topics to negate the graphic ones include the weather, haircuts, sports, and Netflix series.

Talk about the future in positive terms. Reveal your plan to learn to fly fish and how you're gathering information to do so rather than prattle on about how you'll be using your cane to limp to the lake. We find it pointless to talk about what can't be changed or some of the illnesses we've had unless asked. And we've definitely learned with whom to share our illness tales. For example, Barbara learned never to tell one friend about her ailments after she had shared how bad her case of flu was one time and another time what terrible sleep deprivation she had. The friend had experienced each of those maladies far worse—of course! Excessive one-upmanship is draining.

Turn serious ailment-based conversations into humor, if appropriate. Doing so adds levity. If you're discussing the latest gynecological exam, tell a funny story, like the time Margaret was scheduled for one and her usual doctor was unavailable because he was delivering a baby. Another doctor substituted. There she was, legs flailing in the stirrups, when the doctor walked in, sat down to look, and said blithely, "Are you Nolan's wife?" She turned 50 shades of red.

Allow equal time for each speaker. Show the love but don't let them blather on for an hour. Like the woman with the vagina issues, we felt it was time perhaps to initiate a two-to-10-minute rule to leak all . . . and go around the table. Develop a way to monitor time. Now with Zoom for virtual get togethers, the host can mute the speaker after their time is up. If in person, use a stopwatch app on your phone or one that crows: "Time's up." On the other hand, respect each person's point of view by not interrupting or disagreeing during their allotted spiel. Sweetly say, "Next."

Don't prolong discussions by disagreeing. If you think their course of treatment is wrong, don't argue. Listen and don't say a word. Later, you might email or even call to ask if they'd like a suggestion. If they say "yes," explain that you heard about a vastly different procedure for their rotator cuff surgery. Keep in mind that many physicians and other medical personnel disagree about diagnoses, pills, treatments, other doctors, hospitals, and more. Case in point: a woman we know was telling a group of friends her age that she uses fillers to keep her lips puffed, rhapsodizing about how well it works. Hearing this, someone chimed in, "You don't know the side effects? Can't that be dangerous?" It almost caused a world war as the two tangled over whether it was prudent to do this and if it looked attractive.

Don't ask too many questions. Doing so may also prolong conversations. You or someone else might want to ask a few to be polite, but at some point, gently steer away from the conversation and say something to this effect, "I guess we've learned all we can. Maybe we should go for our medical degree if it's not too late."

Establish a penalty. It can be like the political debates. When time is up and the person keeps on talking, give a warning and then start talking over them. Those who don't comply by stopping should know in advance that they'll be penalized by picking up the check, leaving the tip at a restaurant, or doing dishes when the gathering is in a home.

When it's time for problems of real concern, steel yourself to listen. Let the person talk, cry, and ask advice. Give them their 10-minute platform. Try to avoid conversational narcissism such as, "Oh, I had a similar problem. . . ."

Decide how you want to deal with your own illnesses. It's up to you to share what you want, and don't let anyone talk you out of how you plan to proceed, unless it's for valid medical reasons.

Respond to questions firmly. For people who are intrusive, be gentle yet firm. Say some things aren't open for discussion. For those who offer too much advice, again be gentle but firm and say you appreciate their ideas but have your plan. Margaret learned from her front-row seat during her husband's illness which questions she might answer, and which were too painful.

Here's our list of questions to show we care without becoming too intrusive. If the other person offers information, great, but we know to let them take the first step rather than pry:

1. What can I do for your caregiver (husband, partner, friend)?
2. What can I do for you? I mean it and don't say no. Can I bring lunch, take you shopping, walk your dog, take you out for a meal? Choose one.
3. Do you want to talk about it?
4. Is there any kind of advice I might help you research—doctors, at-home nurse, therapist, anything? I can make phone calls for you. I'm eager.
5. I don't want to be a pain but want you to know how much I care. Might I email or text you weekly or call often? What works for you? And if I don't hear from you, that's fine, but do you mind if I check back?
6. Is there a family member who's in charge of a shared email exchange who will let us know how you all are doing, so I don't bother you?
7. Would you prefer that I not share any information you tell me with others or would you like to include a few others to help alleviate some of the work you must do whether research, cooking, driving, walking pets, cleaning, or caregiving? I can always help you set up and manage an online post about your progress on something like CaringBridge.

Listening well is half the equation. That means not having your response or your question ready to fire when the other person is still speaking. Pause, take a breath. Show that you are paying attention by rephrasing what the person has been saying. Example: "I think you said that you need surgery for a female procedure, but at the same time I think you feel this might not be the best time, during the coronavirus, to be in a hospital." This makes the conversation open ended and non-judgmental. It carves out space in the exchange for the person to try to work out a solution herself without being told what to do.

Some responses fail to show compassion or that the person heard your concerns. Among those that tip us off, "Don't worry, it's a nothing procedure. I had that done," or "Your mother's operation will be fine." Well, we wish we felt that way, but we don't always. These types of responses are inconsiderate. They offer no help. It's meant well but . . . the reality can be quite the opposite. It reinforces the fact that the listener hasn't heard your tone and nervousness about the outcome, stay in a hospital, or additional expense.

This conversational dead end concerning our own and family members' and friends' various ailments, organ recitals, house, car, and kid challenges got a head's up from a *New York Times* newspaper article in the Smarter Living section by Anna Goldfarb, titled "Kick Dismissive Positivity to the Curb." We prefer to call this a "false positive"—our riff on a medical procedure that indicates something is present or positive when it's not. That's the good news, but it's not the cheerfulness sought at the time. As Goldfarb wrote, "it's better to respond with something that imparts validation and hope," as well as sincere compassion. We wholeheartedly agree that a sugarcoated dismissive response doesn't hold water. Instead, we'd rather engage in what we term "conversational caring." Example: "I am sure you're feeling nervous about your mother's operation. I wish you the best. I'm here if you need to vent or sound out anything."[1]

When Barbara broke her hand, some tried to make her feel better by saying some variation of "Oh, it could have been worse." Of course, it could have been. She knew she could have hit her head and died as one high-school classmate did before their 50th reunion.

Lynn Marks, 71, has advice about how she wished some of her closest friends and family had dealt with her breast cancer. She now suggests her ideas to others wanting to aid friends if they ask. "Friends can play an incredibly important role by taking the patient to appointments, running errands, taking the kids, bringing food, setting up email trees, being optimistic, or just listening," she says. And she adds, "Don't let the helplessness you may feel prevent you from offering to lend a hand but don't go overboard. Ironically, friends and family can make it more difficult by voicing their fears to the patient. I felt I had to cut off contact with a friend who was pessimistic about my health. That's toxic, I thought. If you want to help, be specific in offering options. It is not as helpful to ask, 'What can I do?' Patients have too many decisions to make as it is. So, if you want to bring food, say, 'I'd like to bring dinner. Do you want chicken or fish?' Offers to loan scarves or hats, and suggestions for television and movies are great. A friend made me a daily schedule of my medications, treatments, and exercise routine. This was extremely helpful since it's easy to get overwhelmed."

Marks also suggests that a friend set up an e-mail chain to convey updates to friends, colleagues, and extended family since writing to each person individually can be taxing and time-consuming. Unless you are close friends, send cards or e-mail messages rather than phone. "It can be exhausting to respond to phone calls, yet the expression of support is invaluable. Most of all, listen to the patient, or partner, or spouse, or grown child fielding calls and emails. Ask for guidance. I didn't have the energy to worry about how my friends were dealing with my illness. There were plenty of times that I didn't want to talk about me or the disease. Remember: you are there to support your friend, not the other way around. For me, nothing is more important than a good friend!"

It's not that we want to hang the black crepe, be the center of attention, and complain endlessly. But those of us who go to the effort of sharing something physically or emotionally painful cherish a response that acknowledges what we face, how we might feel, and that the person being confided in listened.

Our takeaway advice is to avoid rushing in with generalized responses or offering false hope. We have found conversational caring can be contagious in a healthy way, much like when you hand money to a homeless person, others see you and follow suit. Here are steps that represent a good antidote.

1. **Listen and look by offering your full attention.** Don't interrupt and put away your phone.
2. **Show concern.** Offer a shoulder or hug by saying, "I'm so sorry you're nervous about the long recuperation (or surgery). It must be concerning."

3. **Ask relevant questions.** This also helps to show that you want to understand the situation fully but not be too intrusive. "So, the operation involves what? It sounds like you've done your research. I wish you the best." Avoid sensitive questions, such as "Exactly what will be removed?" When one of Barbara's good friends was diagnosed with a medical problem, Barbara was concerned and asked what other doctors said. The friend said she hadn't sought a second opinion. Barbara encouraged her to do so by putting it on herself (i.e., "It was sure helpful when I asked two doctors about a certain minor procedure that was causing my blood calcium to rise. One said to have it done and the other told me to wait. I'm glad I waited"). Barbara's friend got a second opinion at a teaching hospital. The diagnosis and prognosis were far more positive.

4. **Suggest what you might do to help.** Organizing a meal train to have friends deliver lunch or dinner on different nights takes a big concern off their plates. In other cases, write or email a list of helpful names such as a good caregiver if needed or the names of some good books or movies. Consider some that are humorous rather than books or films about people dying in a science-fiction pandemic. Maintain confidences if requested.

5. **Continue support.** Check in periodically to find out how their situation is progressing and if it has been resolved. If not, your friend or family member might need more support. If they're on the mend, time to buy the celebratory bubbly and quaff.

RULES TO FOLLOW IF
YOU NEED A MEDICAL SPECIALIST

We like to be thorough when we deal with a medical challenge, and therefore have created our own playbook of whom to call and where to go:

1. Start with your primary physician or internist or the doctor (specialist) who uncovered the problem, possibly an ob-gyn, endocrinologist, or cardiologist. With a friend or family member in tow, visit the office or participate in a video conferenc-

ing call. Ask what the possible solutions are (e.g., medications versus surgery), and whether additional tests, such as an ultrasound, MRI, or bloodwork are needed to reveal more about the problem. Ask about risks. Take notes or tape record the session. Do not hesitate to ask questions on the spot or jot down questions you might think of later. Also, you can ask questions on the doctor's digital portal if they use one. Check too whether your insurance requires pre-approvals for additional medical visits or tests.

2. Ask for the names of physicians you might consult for a second or third opinion. (You might also ask any friends who are physicians for names of those they know and would recommend.) If your internist says surgery might be needed, you'll next want to consult a surgeon, oncologist, or heart specialist. It can be a doctor who's in proximity to where you live or someone in another city who comes highly recommended.

3. Check credentials and training—where they operate or treat patients, where they received their training, how many years they've been in practice, how many times they've performed the type of procedure or surgery you need, and what their track record of success is. You can also read reviews of many physicians online (with a grain of salt since some disgruntled patients post reviews, too). You may also want to know if the surgeon who might perform jaw cancer surgery and may have to do reconstructive work has a subspecialty in plastic surgery. Do you need an ob-gyn surgeon who has had training in oncology if cancer is a potential problem? Also, if you have a complicated problem, consider if the doctor is affiliated with a major medical center or teaching hospital where cutting-edge research is conducted.

4. Ask your referring physician how soon you should get the second opinion (i.e., within a matter of weeks or a couple months). Also ask how soon you need to be treated—is it an emergency, or can you take more time to research further? Pick one of the names recommended, make an appointment, and have your records sent to that doctor before you meet with them.

5. Find out test results and communicate with your initial doctor and other physicians you've consulted. The portals are good for this, as well as making or breaking appointments, asking for prescription renewals, or simple questions that can be emailed. It's difficult at times to avoid the risk of information overload—and bad news—on these portals, as well as some information you may not understand. If you don't understand what's posted on the portal about a test result, try to stay off the Internet. Instead gather your facts from the doctors when you consult with them in person, during a phone conversation, or via a video conference session. The reason is that not all sites are legitimate or offer up-to-date valid answers, and you may cause yourself unnecessary worry.

6. The day of any appointment with any subsequent physicians, have the same friend or family member go with you again to hear what's being said. Again, draft your list of questions in advance. Write down what's relayed or tape it. Ask what they think the right procedure for your condition is, and again state any risks, and possible side effects. Also ask about the perils of taking a wait-and-see approach or not having the surgery or treatment done at all.

7. Go back and consult with your primary physician or specialist about the results of the second opinion or expert. Some people might get a third opinion if the first two don't agree on the course of action. (Check with your insurance to make sure a third opinion is covered.) However, at some point, you need to stop since all doctors might agree on the problem but arrive at different solutions. Barbara found two surgeons who wanted to treat a recent problem differently; one preferred a much more extensive protocol for preventive reasons.

8. If one of the physicians with whom you consult suggests the wait-and-see approach and you favor that, ask how often you should get more ultrasounds, MRIs, CAT scans, blood work, or whatever's recommended. You want your condition to re-main stable.

9. Weigh all options by making a list of pros and cons. In the end, you are the best person to decide what's right for you.

Chapter Seven

The Things We Do for
Our Kids and Grandkids . . .
While We Try to Come First

When our kids were little, they loved us, listened to us (most of the time), and sought our approval. They'd run and jump, and we'd pick them up and twirl them around. We gave them a hug or kiss and told them how much we loved them. We fed them, clothed them, provided shelter, educated them, and often gave them wonderful summer opportunities such as camps and special trips. If they were rambunctious, we disciplined them. We taught them the importance of doing their chores and impressed upon them their responsibility to be good citizens. We were their role models, inspiration, path forgers. However, we also were faulty and flawed. We did the best that we could and learned the importance of apologizing to them, as we hoped they would do with us.

Now our kids are grown adults, and there are places we can no longer metaphorically go with them. We used to be able to tell them what to do, "Hey, call your favorite aunt who hasn't heard from you in a long time." Or we could be pushier, "Did you forget to write that thank-you note for the present you received?"

For years, we focused on them. As we aged and edged closer to 65 or 70, we flipped the switch to focus on us. We saw a shorter timeline ahead. We yearned for more me time. Jennifer, 57, who lives in Chicago, has found that separation and divorce after a long-term marriage has pushed her to a place she long avoided. "It's brought me to more ME time, and putting myself first," she says, adding, "I just never did this in my life. I went from taking care of my family, then to my husband, and my kids. Now I am enjoying the time to stop, breathe, and answer questions like 'What do I want?' I need to honestly allow myself to finally think about myself. Nobody around ever pressured me not to put myself first, but I just never felt comfortable doing so. Now there is no excuse not to (with the divorce and kids grown). I believe my friendship with my former husband, and the strength of our family even in its new structure, is a result of a more defined, confident me. Everyone benefits from self-love and self-care."

This is so hard to do because these are our kids, not strangers. So, we struggle to find a healthy balance between what we might say and do and the support we offer without usurping their needs and ours.

We also grapple with how much of their advice we should follow as they began to exert themselves more, telling us what to do. At first, we were surprised, then we became used to more debates about this and that and sometimes felt exasperated. During the 2020 coronavirus pandemic, many in our age range found grown children besieged them with loving pleas. "You're in the old age group. You can't go out for anything!" Many of us heeded their counsel and felt good that they cared. However, some felt they overstepped their rights.

The result all proves the point: once children are grown and young adults, it's time to set new boundaries. The old ones are defunct. Yet, we still agonize. How can we share that we want to see them more often than hear their plea for money, and ignore it, unless they legitimately need help? How do we have a conversation about our mortality and discuss how we've set up our estate, which heir or heirs are responsible for our related documents, what's in our will, and who gets what? Do they even want our stuff? Do we allow them to move in with us again or deposit grandchildren at our door so they can enjoy a vacation alone? Aren't we too old to run after toddlers for days? And then, how do we visit our children in their homes and avoid speaking up if behavior of either generation bothers us? We want to be invited back.

Linda K. Stroh and Karen K. Brees, coauthors of *Getting Real about Getting Older: Conversations about Aging Better*, offer tips to come to terms with the fact that our attachment to our children will always be stronger than their attachment to us. "Get really clear on the fact that your children may love you, but there is no way they can love you in the same way you love them. Understand that, consequently, in every interaction, you have more to gain and more to lose."[1]

The biggest struggle may be what power to give them and what to retain before we take our last breaths.

TIME FOR US

Most of us, like Jennifer, have slowly realized that it's our turn to take the wheel firmly in this new landscape of old age rather than be a silent passenger. Family therapist Karen McClelland, LCSW, principal and founder of 911 Help for Parents, is an adolescent, adult, and family therapist in Ellicott City, Maryland. She helped set us straight. "Beware that you are not putting your adult children's needs and wants first, at your expense," she says. To avoid this trap, she emphasizes the importance of educating ourselves on codependency issues. "These include being a helicopter parent, being overbearing/controlling, and doing too much for our children." McClelland stipulates that the stakes change if your adult child has any addictions or physical/mental health issues, or if there are issues stemming from trauma. "Those challenges become important to assess and seek counsel for," she says.

NEW BOUNDARIES WITH ADULT CHILDREN

Toughest for us has been how to stay in our own lane when we want to share our (wise) advice with them. After all, we've lived more than six, seven, or eight decades and know a lot! But in doing so we risk shutting down communication lines, so we keep quiet with a few exceptions. We were reminded of this road map when we read an article in *The New York Times* titled, "A (Short) Guide to Better Boundaries" by Jolie Kerr.

To maintain a healthy journey, we try to let our kids know we still love them, impart some wisdom and experience, try to bite our tongue, and think before we speak. Examples: "What a senseless argument with your wife. Maybe you should apologize!" or "Why don't you consider taking that job since it really might challenge you?" We've learned not to say what we want to, which is: "Did you hear yourself arguing with your spouse? How pointless." Or, "You could have a better job, you know?" Let them make and learn from their own decisions. Then we avoid the "I told-you-so."

At the same time, we learned in a conversation with Ruth Nemzoff, EdD, who holds a doctorate in administration, is resident scholar at Brandeis University Women's Studies Research Center, and author of the books, *Don't Bite Your Tongue* and *Don't Roll Your Eyes*, that holding back is not always ideal. "Kids often know what you're thinking and if left unsaid it can be worse. Especially during the COVID-19 pandemic of 2020, we needed honesty and to be able to talk to each other authentically," she says.

"None of us knows how long we have left, so we should have truthful discussions. The decision to remain silent is different from being silenced," she says. What's more, she adds, is that average lifespans are longer, and we may have more time with our grown children who are now adults than we did when they were kids or young adults. This means we have to try to relate to them differently as we each age. We each go through different stages (both together and separately), which requires flexibility and adjusting our behavior and responses.

Nemzoff offers advice on how best to do this, saying, "Make a conscious decision when to talk and when not to talk. Come clean and share, perhaps, saying, 'There's something that's bothering me. May we talk?'" Know that nothing is perfect in any relationship, so give up that fantasy that you'll do it right all the time. This tack takes practice. "Parenting is more art than science," Nemzoff says. "Be respectful of your children and their choices. Be honest with your feelings. If you are uncertain, ask a close confidante to corroborate or correct your perception. Be ready to ask forgiveness when you err. And, of course, forgive yourself," she says.

We also learned from trial and error to develop tactics based on our different children's personalities and needs. McClelland confirmed that this is prudent. "I think it is very important to recognize that there are many factors operating when it comes to an adult child's needs/wants in terms of boundaries," she says. "These include personality and love language preferences, which means the way we express our feelings of love toward someone that include words of affirmation, gifts, acts of service, doing something special for someone else, quality time, physical touch, developmental stage, cultural constructs, etc." In her experience gender is another factor. "My 22-year-old son much prefers more distance in our relationship than do my daughters—this seems almost evolutionary to me," she says.

For those not sure how to do this, McClelland says to use what seems the most natural parenting for that person. "Look back at your experiences with that child, and the messages they've given you through the years. Ask yourself: Have they given you the message that they want more closeness, more distance? Dependence? Independence? If you are empathically attuned to your child, you will be able to know deeply what they want and need in terms of boundaries," she says.

Barbara learned that one of her daughters wouldn't read long emails. Get to the point, Mom, was her philosophy. She preferred text messages. Margaret's elder son feels the same way. We also know not to expect long phone conversations unless they initiate them for a specific reason. Margaret's daughter doesn't like emails and prefers texts. Her younger son likes to chat on the phone when he's driving in the car or taking a break in his music studio.

Some 20 years ago, when her children were little, McClelland read *Raising Your Spirited Child* and still uses a tip in the book when setting boundaries today. She asks them, "May I give you a suggestion?" "May I give you some feedback? I have found that to be useful." She gives us a snapshot of the boundaries her kids prefer. Typically, she says, one child will roll her eyes, sigh, and say "Sure." Another will say "No, I'm good," and her third will be eager to hear what she has to say. If she steps over the boundary, her kids are quick to let her know.

If you wonder why at times when you text, email, or call there's no response, most likely your kids may not want your input or are too busy to answer. What we don't want to happen is to have them think when our name comes up on caller ID that there's going to be a reprimand or long-winded discourse on something, so they don't pick up, and we feel wounded. Instead, McClelland suggests being patient. Try not to take it personally. "Put yourself in their busy shoes. Keep trying but don't push. Learn how to let go and accept what is. Let them come to you. This is a huge spiritual-emotional task that takes some maturity," she says.

With a lot of practice—and sometimes disappointment, we each are developing ways to set healthy boundaries with our children, now in their mid-30s and 40s. At times it's challenging but has led to good relationships as we heed McClelland's suggestions.

1. **Ask first.** You might say, as she suggests, **"Do you mind if I offer a suggestion?"** If they reply "no," accept their answer. If it relates to their health, try again, with perhaps, "May we talk frankly about something that's a concern for me about your health?" You may get a "no" again, and if so, move on without regret. Or sometimes you'll get a "maybe" and even a "yes." However, just because you speak

your mind with permission doesn't mean the person will take your advice or like it.

2. **Remember, they're still kids.** They probably feel safe calling to vent and complain about a mean friend or awful boss. Listen. They ask us for information that they need to know right now instead of Googling or doing their research. Do your best to provide help when you can. They come to visit and still expect all their favorite foods to be in the fridge—and they are. Feel flattered. They call and say they think they're getting sick and hope for recommendations on remedies or for us to show up on their doorstep with chicken soup— and we do. Oh, the things we swear we won't, yet do, maybe long after we should. We rationalize that they're the only kids we have, and we love them dearly. However, we do know how to say "no" and mean it.

3. **Slow down and think before you speak.** Before you butt in, think about how you would feel if someone usurped the conversation by saying what you're about to ask or say.

4. **Don't explain your decisions.** It works both ways. Our adult kids like to tell us what to do all the time. You don't have to get rude or defensive; it's within the boundary you establish about what you allow in and don't, about what you feel like sharing or not. If they don't like it, that's a shame, but you cannot control their reaction. Say, "I don't want to discuss this."

5. **Communicate in honest, respectful dialogues.** This is key to any relationship. "I often use the 'couples dialogue' method designed by Harville Hendrix, PhD, a best-selling author, which includes how to make requests or file grievances, and teaches the couple how to mirror, validate, and empathize with the other's concerns," McClelland says. She finds that family members often do not know communication 101 skills and should be encouraged to learn them through research, self-help, or professional counsel.

6. **Stick to boundaries you set and be kind.**
   • Say "no" and mean it; it's worse if you backpedal and change your response.
   • Say "yes" and mean it; do what you say you're going to do, especially if it's a promise.
   • Avoid certain topics. If they don't want to talk about their job or love life, respect that.

- Don't say "I'm sorry" unless you mean it and seek forgiveness and let go of the negative energy it takes to be angry or hold a grudge. Grudges are toxic and can spiral out of control.
- Forgive yourself so you don't have to keep saying "I'm sorry," a habit of many women.
- Use "I" rather than "you" messages, as Kerr brought up in her *New York Times* article on boundaries. It's the cardinal rule of good relationship counseling. Tell how you feel. Your kids don't want to be judged and neither do you. When one of Barbara's daughters suggested something she should do for her then 100-year-old mother, Barbara said, "I appreciate your concern, but this is not up for discussion." When feeling cornered or judged, don't engage. Cut off the conversation or change the topic.
- Assess periodically how you're doing. We think we each have good relationships with our children, which we keep working to improve. We recognize they are more independent and have their own lives, friends, careers, and families. We know we're not perfect and recognize this makes our relationships with them authentic. We accept the idea that they may not always think we're so wonderful and could complain to a therapist about how we stifled them in one way or another. We also know we have become more open to hearing criticisms, not sulking, not stopping communications, or hanging up a phone as some of our older relatives have done.
- Master do's and don'ts.

DO . . .
- know your child,
- practice role reversal (imagine you are in their shoes) and ask what they'd want from you as a parent,
- treat each child as an individual with different wants and needs,
- adjust your own needs/expectations accordingly,
- recognize that there are many factors at play in why and how adult children define their boundaries,
- be aware that the developmental stage of individuation is at play and is a necessary part of their healthy growth,
- seek counsel if you hit a wall—either from a mentor who has been through this journey, or from a professional,

- access resources—there are books, articles, podcasts, and Face-book groups on the subject of "grown and flown,"
- attempt to have ongoing conversations with your children when there are bumps in the road and listen,
- accept feedback,
- repair and apologize when appropriate, and
- have self-compassion—you aren't going to do this perfectly and will learn as you go. This is a dance, and you aren't the only one dancing.

DON'T . . .
- take things personally (easier written than followed),
- project your own issues onto your child,
- give up,
- think you're alone,
- minimize how difficult this stage is (it can be quite painful and quite confusing),
- be unconscious (be as intentional and self-aware as possible),
- be ashamed to seek help,
- do too much for them when they are quite capable to at least try in many cases, or
- talk about your children with others who won't keep the confidence; we must respect their confidences and lives.

ADULT KIDS AND YOUR MONEY

Baby boomers spend far more money on their kids than any prior generation. According to a Merrill Lynch and Age Wave study, "More than seven out of 10 parents say they put their children's interests ahead of their own. These parents spend twice as much on adult children (those between ages 18 and 34) adding up to $500 billion a year."[2]

Sometimes, our kids think our love is limitless and so is our money. If they pay the rent, they come to us for help. Do we shell it out? It's not always a good idea to show them the money. If you're stretched financially, don't put your child's financial needs over yours, especially your retirement. It's hard to earn back big bucks at our older stage of life. If you're the financial well and you run dry, that's dangerous for both generations.

Suze Orman, the financial guru and author, warns in "Your 2020 Smart Action Plan" not to hinder their independence by supporting them. Don't get stuck in the "it's only" syndrome. She says, "For each expense you're helping out with, ask yourself whether you're financing a need or a want." She adds, "Your son may want a house. You could help him out, lend him money, but does he really have the financial means to maintain the home?" Probably not a good time to buy yet. Orman adds that if you're helping with rent, keep decreasing the amount you put in each month for a year, then stop. Let them figure it out at that point.[3]

Should you lend your kids money? Mitchell, Missouri trust and estates attorney, cautions it may never get paid back. There are a couple of ways to handle this issue, he says. "First, take a security interest in property that is purchased with the loan, or may already be owned by your child, or relative. For example, some of our clients have funded the purchase of a house for a child with a promissory note at a low interest rate in return and obtain a mortgage, or in Missouri a deed of trust on the home just like a bank would," he says. More often this is generally dealt with in an estate plan upon death of the parent or lender. "If one child has a balance on a loan to be paid back, it makes sense for that to be deducted from what the inheritance would be," he says. To make sure this happens, it's important to put any loans into writing.

These days don't be shocked if your kids want to move back home—for short or long spells. Called "the boomerang generation," these returning adults now include one out of every three Americans between age 18 and 34, according to U.S. Census data. Do you let them live rent free or contribute? Do you require them to help with groceries or chores such as laundry? Do you restrict visits from their friends at odd times? Most experts advise having a plan and boundaries, and sticking with them.

Many kids wanted to return home temporarily during the 2020 COVID-19 pandemic. Some parents permitted them to do so and enjoyed having the generations together; others said "no" for everyone's health. Many parents who welcomed their kids back home have established guidelines. The catch is to get them to listen and have a conversation with feedback on each generation's part. This harks back to communication 101 rules.

Cecilia, 53, a single mother of two sons who lives in New York, is a hair stylist. After her elder son, who was living at home, finished his sophomore year in college, he told his mother one day that he wanted to quit school and go to work. After hearing the news and several minutes of histrionics, Cecilia said she calmed down and said, "I'm a single mother struggling to make ends meet." And then she gave him three options: "1. If you drop out of school and care to live here, you'll have to pay a third of the mortgage, food, utilities, and other household expenses. 2. You are free to move out and live on your own. 3. You may stay in school, graduate, and continue to live at home until you find a job. If you want to still live at home, you'll have to help with expenses." He went to his room and slammed the door. The next morning, after Cecilia spent a sleepless night, she handed him a breakdown of what he would owe if he quit college, went to work, and lived at home. After that sank in, he said, "Okay. I'll go to school for you. That's what you want." He went back to college, finished his degree in computer science, and on graduation day presented his mother with his diploma. A few days later, he found a job with an international bank and moved into his own place. Cecilia's ability to offer him options with consequences was a win-win.

THE DREADED MONEY, INHERITANCE, AND HEALTH PROXY CONVERSATION

Every time Margaret brings up estate planning with her three kids, they say, "We don't want to talk about this. We don't want your money. Spend it on yourself. You deserve it." End of conversation. She was able to get one of her sons and daughter to agree to be coexecutors of her estate and have power of attorney to make health, financial, and other decisions if she becomes incapacitated. However, when it comes to a conversation about specifics like who gets what or how her estate will be divided and why, their eyes glaze over. Forget mention of funeral arrangements and all that entails. Margaret plans to introduce this cautiously, one piece of the conversation at a time, and sooner rather than later.

This is a difficult task. Historically, we didn't have these types of conversations with our parents, so it's new for most people and can feel really uncomfortable. However, Mitchell warns that it's imperative to do good estate planning while we're alive to comply with the complex U.S. estate tax laws and to make sure to avoid excessive taxes on transferring wealth at death, and/or litigation, any of which can result in the worst consequence of all, broken family relationships.

How much can we pass down to heirs without tax consequences? The exemption amount in 2020 without incurring a tax was $11,580,000 per decedent, Mitchell says. "The tax on anything in excess of that amount is 40 percent of the excess amount." Under current law, the estate tax exemption amount is adjusted for inflation and goes up every year.

Once your children are in college, graduated from college, thinking about finances such as starting their first job, an upcoming marriage, or giving birth to a child, experts say, it's wise to tell them about their inheritance in general terms and the way your estate plan works based on your family values. However, the timing of this talk is different for every child. And in the case, heaven forbid, that you're diagnosed with a terminal illness and still able to communicate, it might be the propitious time to tell them as much as you can, no matter where they are in life.

To get advice about how to start the money conversation, we turned to financial planner and wealth advisor Judy Rubin, CFP®, CDFA™, and partner at Plaza Advisory Group, Inc., in St. Louis, Missouri. She advised, before the talk, that you determine the goals and objectives you want to achieve and draft an outline or an agenda with a few talking points. If you have regular family meetings, this is a good time to share the information. If not, then set aside a special time and place to start the talk. Make it as comfortable, secure, and pleasant as possible. Gather your clan together, pick a quiet place, and offer comfort food, hot cocoa, and wine. Decide who you want to include in the meeting, (i.e., spouses of children, for example), since it may impact the direction of the conversation.

Rubin cautions that the first time you have the money conversation, keep the group as small as possible and be very careful when mentioning anything involving death. Your loved ones may find it upsetting to talk about mom's passing so you may need to step into that conversation slowly or in later discussions.

Rubin suggests a dialogue that might be something like this: "I feel that I've given you the best gift of all, your upbringing and education. And you all have done beautifully. Now, I am getting older and want to be able to live the rest of my life the way that I want to and not be a burden on you guys. Plan A is that I live to be 105 without too many health issues, plan B is that I could become disabled or ill, or Plan C is that one day I have a glass of wine, take a nap, and I'm gone with the wind. And someday when that happens, hopefully something will be left for all of you in my estate." Then explain why you set up the plan the way you did. Talk calmly and put it on them. "I'm having this talk for you—it's about your future as well as mine." Let them know this will be the first of several conversations.

Once you decide which individuals you'd like to have any responsibility in your estate planning, you should ask and then confirm that they are willing and able, says Rubin, who adds that it's best to spell out why you've chosen this person (or persons) and (depending on the task) give them the tools that they will need. "For example, if you appoint someone to make medical decisions for you, that person needs a copy of the signed document that gives them authority. He or she will also need to keep it somewhere handy because when there's a health crisis, time is of the essence. Years ago, I knew an attorney with two aged parents who kept copies of his parent's documents in the trunk of his car for quick access. Nowadays, we can save these documents within a vault or safe deposit box, on a computer, or in 'the cloud.'"

One thing adult children do not need to know, even if they are responsible for your estate, are specific dollar amounts that they might inherit. It's because these totals might change, depending on when you pass away and tax laws at that time. Mitchell also is opposed to showing them specific documents unless the child has power of attorney for financial matters and health care and you want them to know that. The document is irrevocable and is intended to benefit the child immediately (this disclosure is likely required by law anyway; it is in Missouri). "Most estate planning documents are revocable and can change. Therefore, summaries are fine. The concepts behind why a plan is structured the way it is are less likely to change than the actual documents, which might be revised to account for changes in law from time to time," Mitchell explains.

If these meetings become unpleasant, don't argue, or shut down. Let everyone have a say. Try to listen. If an uncomfortable issue comes up, try to have an answer, or say, "Let me think about that. I'll have to get back to you, but it's a good question." Also, it might be prudent to have an advisor present. Mitchell feels whether a neutral party is needed really depends on the complexity of the plan and the amount of wealth involved.

At the root of these estate planning conversations is how you plan to divide your assets. This is when you should let your kids know who will receive what—insurance payouts, investments, and property or business interests. You certainly don't need to tell everyone exact details and you shouldn't give them the impression that anything can be predicted with certainty. You don't want your kids to be counting on inheriting a million dollars and then actually inherit a small amount due to unexpected future expenses or investment failures. Also, be transparent in terms of all others to whom you might be leaving money such as a sibling, niece, or charity. Tell the kids the division of your assets is going to be as equal as you can make it based on your family's value system, advises Rubin, but be aware that it can sometimes be difficult to make it equal.

Some of your children might have different levels of need. In this case, do you divide your estate equally? It's your decision but explain why you made your decisions. You don't want the trust and will to be read after you're gone and the kids to find out that their brother is inexplicably getting more. This can unleash a torrent of emotions and initiate a will contest. Rubin cautions, "Even if one child disappoints you in some way, please never say to them, 'I'm going to take you out of my will.'" We know a man whose father would regularly threaten to do so if his son didn't call home once a week when he was in graduate school or pick a profession his parents wanted him to choose. Be careful about using money or inheritance as a carrot or a whip, says Rubin. "It can ruin relationships. I can't imagine retaliating after death. This tactic will speak long after you're gone." After you've had this discussion, stick to your decision. If you make a change, host another meeting for all to attend.

Mitchell emphasizes that touchy subjects like your health care, elder care, and family values are even more important than disclosing how someone's inheritance is going to work. If you can't talk to your child about your health care choices, faith, values, or mission, you might not want to disclose the structure of an estate plan.

It's critical that you have a living will and someone in charge of your health care. You don't want your kids to fight over what to do with you in a near-death situation. Margaret has a friend who told her recently that she called a funeral director, arranged her entire funeral, and paid for it. She's neither ill nor dying. However, she's thinking ahead and does not want her only child, who works for her ex-husband, to have to handle this in a crisis and risk her ex usurping her son's power. "I'm doing this for my peace of mind." Have you discussed this with your son yet? Margaret asked. "Not yet. I have to find the right time." As for her health proxy, her son, and a close family friend, are both on it.

Elder care can be another unpleasant topic. But address it. Do you prefer to live in a retirement or senior community, assisted living or nursing home, or plan to age in place in your own home or in a cohousing community? Include in your discussion your end-of-life wishes. If hospice is needed, do you want it at home or in a hospital? Where do you want to be buried? Have you purchased a plot? It's smart business to spell this out earlier rather than later. You can set aside money in your retirement accounts or use long-term care insurance to finance the costs for all, so you don't put a financial burden on your kids or heirs.

Robert, a retired physician, says he did not purchase long-term care insurance. "I decided long ago that it was too expensive, not reliable enough, and I would rather 'self-insure' with my own savings. It would not have been very helpful for my wife's long illness and would not have been flexible enough to cover the six or seven ladies who I hired privately to work in our home," he says.

On the other hand, in the 1990s, Stricker and her husband, who have no children, did. "We purchased long-term care insurance through my husband's former company. We had friends who lived through a house explosion that incapacitated them for months, so we took a cue from that. We thought if we get sick now and have to go into a facility for a while, we're going to need to have some extra insurance. My mother also had long-term care insurance, and it was a blessing. It covered about half her monthly costs to live in assisted care."

After the discussions, you may want to have an attorney draft a summary of your estate, will, health, and elder care plans, and distribute it to your heirs. And again, those who have a role in the future management of your estate should have full copies of all documents just in case. You'll also want to include where your important documents are located. Then, hold another family meeting to review the documents and answer questions. Be prepared for some tough ones.

GIFTING MONEY TO FAMILY WHILE ALIVE

Giving away money during your lifetime is one way to reduce estate taxes. However, warns Mitchell, "If you give a gift that isn't excluded from gift tax, the amount you give reduces your remaining estate tax exemption amount dollar for dollar." He explains that you cannot give away everything before you die, or the tax consequences will be enormous.

The simplest technique to avoid gift tax consequences is the annual exclusion gift tax (which in 2020 was $15,000 to each heir) to as many different people as you desire without it reducing your gift/estate tax exemption amount. Mitchell explains that if you have five children, at $15,000, you can give $75,000 away among them equally with no transfer tax consequence. If you're married, your spouse can also do the same, which totals $150,000 each year. Mitchell adds, "What you do depends on how many heirs, dependents, the makeup of your assets, and factors you cannot control such as the economy—what assets and real estate are worth and current interest rates. If low, it makes good sense to make family loans."

WHAT ABOUT A 529 PLAN?

When you give to a 529 plan for education, you can get money out of your estate by lumping five years into this plan as a one-year gift. In other words, you can gift $75,000 ($150,000 if you're married) to each of your beneficiaries' 529 plans this year (2020) with no gift or estate tax consequences, says Mitchell. You can always take out your contribution amount from a 529 with no federal income tax consequences (because you put in after-tax money), but if you take more than your contribution out you have to pay the income taxes on the earnings above your contribution amount plus a 10 percent penalty. This can be waivable in some cases such as your child receiving a scholarship of an amount high enough to justify you taking out even earnings from the 529, he says.

"Another 'simple' strategy used for wealthy individuals to reduce their estate is to give away property having a value equal to the gift/ estate tax exemption amount as soon as possible so that its appreciation and income earned after it is given away is no longer in the giver's estate," says Mitchell. These strategies and more complicated ones that involve discounts in the valuation of the property given away for gift tax purposes are best discussed with your finance and legal professionals.

ROTH IRA

These are a wonderful vehicle for investment savings during your life since they have benefits, according to Mitchell. They do not require any required minimum distributions during life. None of the withdrawals from a Roth account is ever taxed, during life or after death. Investments in Roths grow tax free too so many people take advantage of these accounts for as long as they can. One disadvantage is that they have a low limitation on contributions each year relative to other lifetime estate tax planning techniques.

Mitchell says they must be funded by the owner, but that does not preclude you giving money to a child to fund a Roth so long as the child has earned income in that amount and the child doesn't already fund a Roth on their own. "In 2020, the maximum contribution the child can make to a Roth IRA, whether the money is his own or received from a parent, is the lesser of $6,000 or his earned income. Persons also become ineligible to make Roth IRA contributions after a threshold level of income ($139,000 for a single person or $206,000 for a married couple)." Ways of doing this are complicated and Mitchell recommends professional guidance here as well.

A rule of thumb is that after age 59½, you can take as much as you want out of a Roth with no tax or penalty. However, there are penalties for withdrawing earnings before age 59½ best spelled out by a professional. Rubin suggests that before taking out distributions at any age or even at the allotted age of 59½ you know the rules to avoid penalties governing your unique situation. And remember the benefits of leaving the money invested in that type of account for as long as you can, if you can. Consult your banker or tax professional. "While you can take money from a Roth IRA, you could be subject to some tax if you haven't fulfilled certain requirements or if the withdrawals fail to qualify for distribution exceptions," says Rubin. Here is a hyperlink to the IRS document: https://www.irs.gov/publications/p590b#en_US_2019_publink1000208. This is a bit complicated, which is why you should get advice if you can.

Some parents or grandparents opt to pay for everyone's college education out of pocket. Rubin says this can get tricky. "What if the grandparents die before the youngest goes to college and there is no money left or provisions in place in the estate to pay for schooling?" Mitchell concurs but reminds us that direct payments for tuition and medical care are not treated as gifts. "They don't even reduce the annual exclusion amount available to give to a child without using lifetime gift/estate tax exemptions. Family loans, another simple technique that charge a proper interest rate, are also not treated as gifts so long as there is not an understanding in advance that they never have to be paid back," Mitchell says.

A WILL AND WAY FOR ALL YOUR STUFF

It's wise while you're alive that you and your adult children discuss who will get your personal property, including items of sentimental value. This helps alleviate surprises and arguments among heirs. Some may soon arise but know you can't control people's reactions.

Some will be delighted to take hand-me-downs. However, don't be surprised if your adult children tell you they don't want most of your possessions. They may say, "We have nowhere to put it. We live in much smaller places than you do." They may avoid saying, "It isn't our taste." Accept their decision and leave it at that or bring it up a year later if their status changes and they marry or have a child. They might change their mind.

Margaret made big decisions along these lines before moving to New York City. She thought that her children might want something small, personal, or meaningful. "How about one item?" Margaret convinced her daughter to take her first-married set of dishes. With her elder son, she was pushy about his taking her late husband's Parson's desk that her son reluctantly stuck in the living room of his apartment. "I think it looks terrific," she told him. He's more pragmatic, telling her that the desk is a good resting place for a much-needed lamp to brighten the room. And this spring with the coronavirus scare and having to work from home, he relished having the desk for work.

Her younger son helped her sort through their extensive record collection and took some records, along with sheet music and instruments. What he wanted and had no place for was the family Steinway piano. Her elder son encouraged a friend to keep the piano for now.

Barbara's daughters echo similar sentiments. Her younger daughter's older son is likely to be gifted her baby grand piano since he's already enchanted with music. Her older daughter wants her handcrafted mahogany breakfast table and six chairs; she also wants her grandmother's book collection. Both girls are being gifted Barbara's and her mother's good china sets, crystal, and silver sterling flatware "someday." And they may want some artworks. Each also will take the oil portraits that were painted of them when they were 3 years old. It's unlikely much else will appeal, especially not the American Girl dolls she's stored in multiple attics for more than 30 years.

At the same time, we recognize that our adult children cherish their childhood memories and may take photos of the actual stuff since this generation tends to digitize almost everything.

Just in case they might change their minds and decide they want something before you sell, donate, or give away things, McClelland suggests announcing to offspring that you are designating a day to set everything out for them to look through (or send photos or video conference). It's a last call. Set a date that is several months out (if possible) so everyone has time to participate. Give them a deadline.

VISITING OUR ADULT KIDS AND GRANDKIDS AND BEING INVITED BACK

Visiting with our kids and grandkids can be wonderful or fall apart if certain boundaries aren't maintained. Yes, those boundaries again. It's tempting when getting together to switch back into a parental role. "Please don't slam the door." Or there are, of course, the lights they leave on. McClelland suggests how we can make these visits amicable:

- practice open communication;
- hear what they have to say and be empathetic;
- be proactive and set up social contracts beforehand;
- if possible, to literally avoid stepping on each other's toes and make these visits pleasant, have separate space (i.e., the basement); and
- after you leave, assess how it went and adjust to do things better next time.

Barbara, who has two young grandsons in another city, stays with them when visiting. Her daughter has a guest suite on a different level than the other bedrooms, which gives generations privacy. Because she wants the visit to go well, she balances helping without being intrusive. These were her rules before the 2020 coronavirus pandemic, which she hopes she'll soon get to follow:

1. **Come when the parents are in need.** They may have a meeting out of town, are sick, or their child may have a day off from school, and there's no back-up care.
2. **Bring something for the younger generation.** Barbara's daughter thinks her mother has created a monster by always having presents in tow. The two grandsons always ask when she visits, "What'd you bring me?" She's from the school that believes spoiling the boys is part of her birthright.
3. **Try to help.** Barbara tries to help by cooking meals during the weekdays when the parents work.
4. **Play with the kids.** That usually means writing an original story with her older grandson and illustrating it together with magic markers or paints or just painting together.
5. **When up, feed and play.** Barbara is an early riser, so this helps. Sometimes, she'll just read a book quietly to her grandsons, though they've also gone out for a walk.
6. **Observe parents' no-screen rule.** Stay off your cell phone and laptop as much as possible. Don't turn on the TV unless you ask the parents' permission. Barbara tries to heed these rules even for news unless the kids are asleep and only if her daughter and son-in-law approve.
7. **Never criticize your children's choices or get angry at their kids.** Caveat: if the kids are in any kind of danger, then it's smart to speak up and act quickly.

8. **Don't butt in.** When her daughter and son-in-law talk, she doesn't add her two cents, unless asked.
9. **Limit the stay.** Make your stay short. As the saying goes: guests and fish start to smell after three days, especially if you start to become judgmental of their apartment or home. In between visits, FaceTime and Zoom often and write postcards or letters.
10. **Help clean up.** Barbara tries to help straighten up toys and books and leave her guest bedroom and bathroom tidy.
11. **Do something special.** Barbara has found a restaurant in her daughter's neighborhood they love and takes her older grandchild and his parents to dinner. They sit at the counter and schmooze with staff. She also offers to babysit so her grown kids can go out alone, and she walks her older grandson to school or picks him up.

Two of Margaret's grown children, who do not have kids, live in other cities; here are rules she follows.

1. **Make the bed in the morning.**
2. **Do not leave the bathroom a mess.**
3. **Ask how to work the appliances** if you plan to use them. If not, you might be paying for repairs.
4. **Turn off lights, lock doors, and do not leave the stove on.**
5. **Do not eat them out of house and home.** Do the grocery shopping and get, at the very least, eggs, milk, bread, and other staples. If you're planning to cook a nice dinner at home, buy the food and offer to help cook.
6. **Do not expect to be waited on.** This is not a hotel or restaurant.
7. **Take the family out while you're there to treat them.**
8. **Replenish anything that you use** such as their shampoo, Kleenex, or any foods.
9. **Do things on your own.** Your kids are not a travel agency or personal Uber service. Get around using public transportation, cabs, or a drive share.
10. **If they give you an extra key to use while you're there, remember to return it.**
11. **Send a thank you email, handwritten note, or gift.**

If your adult kids visit you, set house rules in advance

Now let's turn the tables. Whether your daughter and her husband or partner or your son and his fiancé and a gaggle of kids—your precious grandkids—come to visit, you'll be excited to say the least. The catch is that you're not used to having anyone in your space unless you're married or in a relationship. Suddenly, the group who are all much younger descend on your turf. You like order. You have a routine. You're not used to regular mealtimes anymore. But all that is superseded by the fact that you can't wait to see them, especially if it was during the 2020 COVID-19 pandemic when so many kept their distance to stay healthy.

Whenever you're together, remember our advice. Don't be a doormat. And that's why it's smart to have the rules in place before they knock on the door and announce, "We're here."

1. **Determine length of stay ahead of visit.** Shorter is better—two or three days unless they've come from far away.
2. **No one leaves dishes, glasses, and other stuff in the kitchen sink.** At least know they're to wash or rinse and put them in the dishwasher. In the morning, it's nice if someone steps up and empties the dishwasher and puts away clean dishes rather than waiting for you to do it.
3. **Set mealtime hours.** Your home is not a diner where they can expect a meal any time.
4. **Set aside space in your refrigerator for their favorite foods**, some of which you might buy and others they'll have to purchase when they get to your home. You don't have to buy everything.
5. **Remind them—and many dislike this—that utilities can be expensive.** They should turn off lights when they leave a room. They shouldn't take excessively long showers. They should close doors and windows, especially in summer when bugs fly inside and air conditioning escapes!
6. **They shouldn't touch anything without asking**, especially changing the heat or air conditioning temperatures.
7. **If they need to do laundry, show them how to use the machines.** Same with the dishwasher, coffee machine, and outdoor grill. Be sure there are some empty drawers and shelves where they can place their clothing. Be sure they know where to find extra blankets, towels, and pillows.

8. **Let your kids know when you plan to go to bed and get up** and if you have any errands to run. They should be quiet when you want to sleep.

9. **If your grown kids want to go out, tell them the time by which you'd like them to be home**, if that matters at all. Coming in too late might wake you up—or not. If you use an alarm system, give them the code.

10. **Make a list of activities you can do together and what you need to do alone**—maybe you're still working and are on deadline. You should spend some quality time having fun!

11. **Ask in advance if they have any expectations regarding foods or meals** they want to help with or activities they want to do, which might include seeing childhood friends if they grew up in the area. You're likely to be exhausted when they leave, so get some rest. Know that next time, although the visit was great fun but not perfect, you'll always welcome them with open arms, especially if they follow some rules.

CONUNDRUM OF GROWN STEPKIDS OR PARTNER'S GROWN CHILDREN

Wouldn't it be wonderful if real life played out like the old sitcom *The Brady Bunch*. In TV land, everyone's kids got along splendidly, almost like real siblings; they also fought, too, which was normal and healthy.

It doesn't always happen that way for a variety of reasons: worry over a future inheritance; jealousy about the other kids being liked better or spending more time with the couple; different ways of doing things based on how they were raised; or simply a grab for power, ego, or insecurity.

How do you deal with such a challenge? Trying not to replace a mother or father, whether lost through divorce or death, is a good way to start. Giving the partner enough time alone with their kids is another essential. Not criticizing the kids to the other parent is another rule, sometimes tough, especially when they're rude behind or in front of you. Accepting what may be—and that some kids will never like you or your offspring—is crucial.

What can be done if you're in a romantic relationship, not married, your partner with kids gets seriously ill and is hospitalized, and the kids refuse to let you see their father or mother? Or the one partner dies, and the other partner is not allowed to attend the funeral? Is there a document that can be drafted and signed to prevent this from happening? Rubin says these are questions that should be directed to an attorney. "Marriage affords us all certain rights and lacking that, couples can draft legal documents to try to protect each other as best as possible. In fact, if two people are committed to one another but cannot marry for whatever reason, I recommend that they actively engage in estate planning to try to solve questions like these and others. For instance, I personally know one man who was kicked out of the condo owned by his partner [the condo was passed down to the kids in his estate] after the partner suddenly died of a heart attack. Good planning could have prevented that," she says.

Robert and Edward have lived together for four years. The two, each of whom has children, are thinking about marriage but have many issues to address. Among them: Do we have a prenup before marrying, and what would it say? What are the pros and cons of marrying? Robert says that one of the advantages of doing so are the financial, tax, and health benefits. On the other hand, he says, getting married creates new issues such as what to do about estate planning. "My son is executor of my will and has my health proxy and power of attorney. How would I change my estate plan to include my husband?" he asks.

Most important, don't allow kids to come between you and your partner. Proper planning will help. And if things go awry in the relationship because of the kids, consider counseling. As one therapist told someone we know having a difficult time with self-centered, angry grown children of their partner, "You're the one he comes home to and sleeps with; remember that."

SERIOUS ILLNESS AND DEATH DISCUSSION

Some families hide secrets at every stage, including serious and terminal illnesses, even from grown children. Margaret's late husband, Nolan, didn't want his children, two of the three of whom lived away, to worry. He thought it would be best to sugarcoat his cancer. "I'm doing fine," he would say when two of the kids called home. He forbade Margaret from telling the kids otherwise. In retrospect, Margaret felt she had to honor his wishes but regrets keeping the facts from the kids. It did make them angry, especially because the true story was shared too late, when her husband was near the end of his life. It makes grown children feel like they are so fragile that they're unable to help make decisions and handle life's tough parts. This can be a very harmful lesson that they carry through life. Think about such decisions long before they're needed so each generation has input.

PRACTICE MAKES PERFECT ENOUGH

For generational relationships to thrive, respect is a two-way street. This can prove tough at times, and we may veer in a direction our children may not like, and vice versa. It's important to keep lines of communication open and work on what works best for all. As McClelland shares, practice makes perfect or perfect enough, regardless of the endeavor.

Chapter Eight

Inventory Your
Work Life before Retirement

By the time we've hit our older years, most of us rethink or have re-thought our work lives. Do we go, stay, or start something new?

For some, the idea of a retirement always appealed. For others, it connoted emptiness and boredom. Those people imagined missing the activity and satisfaction that's associated with building, working in, or running a company. They may also miss the money.

In our case, we remain passionate about what we do and see no reason to stop. Feeding into this is the fact that we expect to live longer and hope we remain healthy. One hundred years ago, we were lucky to live to be age 50. Now, people live to be 100-plus. It is estimated that there were 82,000 centenarians in the United States in 2016 and will be 589,000 by 2060, according to statista.com.[1]

A physician friend of Barbara's at a teaching/research hospital says he has no plans to stop work, even though he's in his mid-70s. His hospital has required him to scale back, and he knows he may curtail surgery to train more young doctors. "I love what I do," he says with enthusiasm. He still finds time to run, which is another passion.

Retirement is also not on Princess Anne of England's agenda, though she, too, is in her 70s, according to an article, "A Royal Spark," by Katie Nicholl in *Vanity Fair* magazine. "I don't think retirement is quite the same (for me). Most people would say we're lucky not to be in that situation because you wouldn't want to just stop," she said.[2]

We feel the same way about our work as freelance writers—not about every assignment but many, and certainly our weekly blog posts and the books we coauthor. So, we keep going at times like a couple of windup toys as long as we enjoy what we do and find publishers to showcase our writing. We also like the funds we earn, engaging with others even if by phone or email, learning about others' lives through our relentless questioning, and mastering new technologies that our assignments require. Our work keeps us engaged and makes our lives more interesting.

For those who appreciate the benefit of working together like we do, we have found it's a way to circumvent the loneliness and solitude that otherwise might have happened. This was especially invaluable during the coronavirus pandemic of 2020. The feedback we offer each other is honest and invaluable. "Why did you write it this way?" or "What were you thinking?" one of us will email. We're a well-oiled team after 30-plus years.

We are also lucky we can still laugh uproariously at the pickles we've been in as well as how some tough CEOs have teared up during our "interrogations." We recall when we prepared a marketing brochure for the Zaca Mesa Winery in Los Olivos, California, and were told this would involve camping. We both feared sleeping in a tent. Despite our trepidation, no bugs or snakes got us, but the chorus of snoring men in an adjacent tent kept us up. That was offset, however, by the pre-glamping tents we stayed in, our meals prepared by a gourmet chef accompanied by wonderful wines, and the offer to try hang gliding, which we politely declined. A tough camping experience? Hardly.

We know we may be the exception to keep chugging along in our 70s. Sometimes, we feel like we're climbing a steep hill—in our case finding new assignments as the number of print publications dwindles. But we stick it out and often go in a different direction with our writing assignments, perhaps do more editing for clients, write for websites, add more frequent blog posts, or write press releases for others. At the same time, we watch and listen as friends, family, and work colleagues our age embark on different types of work or cut the work cord swiftly and enjoy time spent playing cards, Mahjong, golf, traveling, cooking, and babysitting grandchildren.

As we've considered options and listened to stories, we think there's no single answer regarding when to stop. An active, healthy businessman, "Paul," who lives in Chicago, continues to work at age 83. "Working keeps my mind and my body active," he says.

Others craft new careers or fill their lives with a hobby or passion, and others end their careers for emotional, physical, financial, collegial, health, or other reasons. Some experience separation anxiety and depression at no longer going into an office and being "needed." And some go through a phased transition to test full retirement. Barbara's ob-gyn stopped performing surgery but still saw patients until she decided to retire at age 62. A writer friend of Barbara's stopped taking assignments that require more than one rewrite. A lawyer friend quit completely to focus on exercise and volunteering. Everybody has their reason and way to fill time but not everyone has finetuned a plan. We consider some planning wise even if changes occur during retirement.

A man Margaret interviewed had been a metals trader who retired, as he liked to say, "to nothing." He tried to stay busy exercising, reading, helping with his 10 grandchildren, and serving as a consultant to his son-in-law's trucking business. However, he needed a second act. Then one night on TV, he heard about the plight of refugees around the world. It resonated. Today he has poured his money, empathy, energy, passion, and persistence into a nonprofit that resettles refugees in the United States. He is one of countless people over age 50 who is reimagining themselves.

Also, after last year's horrendous financial hit due to the 2020 COVID-19 pandemic, who knows how many of us can't stop work and must seek new ways to earn income—fast. Some walk dogs, babysit, serve as nannies, work in a retail store, bartend, or waitress. A TV sports cameraman who had no work or income in his field during the pandemic found an interim job at Amazon.

Ken Dychtwald, PhD, retirement expert, and author, encourages retirees in his new book, *What Retirees Want: A Holistic View of Life's Third Age*, to look for meaningful ways to fill their time when they retire. Here are some suggestions based on our and others' ideas.

STEP AWAY COMPLETELY

Many we know have found that the later years are a time to leave in one decisive step, like the metals trader. Maybe, work became exhausting and required too many hours or took an emotional toll. Maybe, demanding clients or colleagues made the job less than joyful. Maybe, it became too hard to keep up on new trends and technologies, one of the reasons Margaret's mother stepped down in her late 60s from a successful real estate agent job. Or maybe, the workplace had an age limit that required retirement.

According to an August 28, 2020, piece in the *New York Times*, "When Retirement Comes too Early," by Paula Span, during the 2020 COVID-19 pandemic, "The New School's Retirement Equity Lab reported in early August that 2.9 million workers ages 55 to 70 had left the labor market since March [2020]—meaning that they were neither working nor actively job-hunting—and projected that another 1.1 million might do so by November."[3] Suddenly, many folks 50-plus had to scramble to find new work at an almost impossible time to do so or consider retirement if they could afford it. Some were forced to start new careers or take any job they could get. There were many scenarios.

Brooklyn, New York-based architect "Emma," 71, worked for 40 years after graduating from architecture school with a master's degree. After joining a few firms for specific projects, she settled in at a company that specialized in healthcare design and focused on designing hospitals, labs, medical office buildings, and more. Eventually, she started her own firm in this niche. She made additional moves and progressed up the career ladder, taking work that included budgeting, building layouts, and managing projects. In the final years of her career when she was with a major metropolitan healthcare corporation, funding was cut, and work became political and bureaucratic.

Although her career overall had been fulfilling, after several years of debate, she couldn't believe "how glad I was to finally leave this work environment behind." She consulted a financial planner, her romantic partner, close friends, and family and decided that, with the pension, savings, and Social Security benefits, she'd be alright. Her only regret was leaving close colleagues behind.

To mark the milestone, she and her partner took a six-week road trip west, something neither had done for years. Once back, she decided to keep her options open, based on advice from her older sister, who said, "Don't fill your time. Let your days be free and see where your mind and heart wander." She also watched how her partner spent his time since he had retired before she did.

Her new routine is to rise and enjoy a leisurely breakfast, read the newspaper, exercise, help with her partners' grandkids, visit with friends, cook more, see museum exhibits, sing in a chorus, travel, and regularly visit her son and his family on the West Coast for extended stays. She regularly volunteers for political campaigns and works in her neighborhood food co-op. She's also guided friends through their renovation projects. Though she saw work expenses disappear, new ones popped up, including expensive dental work and unexpected house repairs. She knows she has the safety net of renting out a second bedroom in her Brooklyn cooperative apartment. "Initially, I felt anxious, but it's all working out, and I'm prepared for the inevitable ups and downs that occur," she says. "Most of all, I am glad to be healthy and able to enjoy life."

The change to retirement can also be gradual as industry practices and technologies evolve or health takes a turn and priorities change. That happened with Chicagoan Lauren, 70, who studied teaching hearing impaired students in college and worked in that field until her two children were born. Coincidentally at that time, a new parenting publication run by mothers was launched in Chicago, and she was asked to help sell advertising. "I had never, ever, considered that field, but it offered flexible hours and permitted me to work from home, even from my car," she says.

After working for the publication for several years, another advertising job became available after she spied an ad in a newspaper for a salesperson for a new bridal publication. She got the job to place ads in its Chicago version and found she loved it. "I was once again able to work from home and was diligent about doing it. So many would ask if I watched any of the TV soaps, got dressed, made my bed, and so on. I was very self-disciplined and thrived. I never turned on the TV, threw in a load of wash, and rarely took a break outside for lunch. I even went back to my home office at night to finish paperwork and other parts of the job. I also never felt lonely since I was on the phone all day pitching ads. If necessary, I could get to my kids' school events or activities."

A year or two after a major surgery 11 years ago, she decided to retire. "Advertising had evolved and changed. Print was taking a hit, there was a change in management at my company, and I simply wasn't enjoying the work as much. My former boss started his own business, which was a different model, and I went to work for him for a while. However, my heart just wasn't in it, and I decided—after also talking to my husband—that it was time to step away, unless something part-time came up. My husband was still working, and we could afford to give up my salary and travel a bit more. Our two grown children lived away."

Since her full retirement, Lauren has filled her time with travel, including visiting 49 of the 50 states—Alaska is still to come, postponed because of the coronavirus of 2020. "I'm really a frustrated travel agent and love researching trips." She and her husband are also in a variety of groups or clubs for movies and international cooking, and they subscribe to different theater programs and attend the symphony. On her own, Lauren's in a book group, takes classes at Northwestern University, is in an art appreciation group, and is taking a short-story class. Several years ago, her husband went to part-time work and recently retired, though he was asked shortly afterward to come back twice weekly to help mentor younger doctors. As she looks back on her 41-year-work career, she has no regrets.

SWITCH TO PART-TIME

Some prefer to test retirement with a part-time variation, maybe to continue to earn money or keep a hand in their field so they don't become rusty, lose touch with colleagues and technology, or stop stimulating their brain.

Nancy A. Shenker, 64, created an interim stage that she calls "pretirement." Describing herself as high energy and someone who loved her work as a marketing consultant (virtual chief marketing officer/CMO) and business writer, she can't imagine stopping completely after decades as a "C" or corporate-level executive. After moving about two years ago to Scottsdale, Arizona, from Minneapolis, which had been preceded by decades of living and working in the New York City area, she decided she needed to devote more time to caring for herself and having fun. "I raised two daughters, who live in the Washington, DC, area, am divorced, and felt it was time for me to explore options, relax, and try new things while I still am healthy rather than do just what other people need," she says.

She chose Arizona rather than somewhere on the East Coast because of the lower cost of living, glorious weather, and having a mother in her 90s living in Tucson. She takes off most Fridays but still works to bring in an income to maintain a certain quality of life she was accustomed to and keep her brain active. Knowing how to network to make new friends and business contacts, she quickly settled into a routine that keeps her happy.

"I'm good at waking up early to meet deadlines and then go out for a bike ride, lift weights, or do something else I enjoy, which includes writing my blog posts," she says. One blog site, www.bleisureliving.com, fulfills her love of travel; www.embracethemachine.com feeds her passion for "human-centric technology," and another, www.theonswitch .com, helps build her business. She also writes for Thrive Global and other lifestyle and business media. And she's made at least five friends—from their 20s to their 70s, she says, who she knows care enough about her well-being that she could call any to drive her to and from a colonoscopy, the ultimate friendship test in her book. Eventually, she plans to stop accepting less appealing work and indulge herself more. Maybe, she'll completely retire, though that's not on the immediate horizon.

TEST A NEW CHALLENGE

Others switch to something related to the work they once did but in a more casual, maybe pro-bono way. Doing so gives them greater control over their time or a renewed sense of meaning at this later stage in their life.

Lynn Marks, a public interest attorney in Philadelphia, Pennsylvania, for more than 40 years, decided almost four years ago it was time to move on. She stepped down from a 25-year job as executive director of a statewide nonprofit organization. Throughout her career, she had directed nonprofits: advocating for changes in the justice system, increasing public awareness of issues, and organizing coalitions. She's worked on court reform, gender/racial bias in the justice system, violence against women, homelessness, reproductive rights, and breast cancer. Itching to get back to hands-on involvement in programs and administration, she thought, what could she start that was new and different but would still involve her passion for justice as well as curiosity for hearing varying perspectives?

That's when she started teaching a 1½ hour weekly class with a respected retired judge called "Hot Topics in Justice and Law" to adults over age 55. They teach through a local university in Philadelphia. Initially, 400 people signed up, but they could only take 100. Had she kept working in a demanding full-time job, she might never have started this new phase.

Each week they explore current policy and legal issues with expert speakers from opposing perspectives. "Hot topic" ideas include discussions on immigration, reproductive freedom, sanctuary cities, criminal justice reform, the Me Too movement, presidential powers, voting reforms, and LGBTQ issues, to name a few. Speakers for the class have included political and community leaders, reporters, authors, judges, government reformers, pollsters, and pundits. Among those have been Edward G. Rendell, former governor of Pennsylvania, the mayor of Philadelphia, former head of the DNC, and an MSNBC political commentator. In one class at the beginning of last semester, they had the head of the state chapter of the ACLU and the head of the Federalist Society both talk about their agendas for the year.

Marks says that teaching this class gives her the opportunity to remain part of the social justice community. The students, who are retired doctors, lawyers, teachers, journalists, et al., are hungry for information to keep their minds sharp and are excited to be presented both sides of hot topics. "It's really rewarding when the students come up to us after class to tell us how much they've learned," she says. During the pandemic of 2020, the two taught their class online. More recently, on a part-time basis, she started leading an initiative of the local courts in Philadelphia to figure out how to get more African Americans into the jury pool.

FORGE A NEW PATH

Some use their newfound time to do something different from what they did in their careers but which they may have long wanted to pursue. They might work in a bookstore because they're an avid reader and like customer contact, maybe open a bakery after years of making cookies and cakes at home and getting raves from friends, or become a professional musician after playing for years and performing in recitals. Some of these new ventures feed souls and stomachs more than bank accounts, though second and third careers can generate significant dollars. The founder of Coach Leatherware went on to start Coach Farm, and many restaurants and grocery stores buy its goat cheese products.

Amy Gewirtz, in her early 60s and living in suburban New York, was an attorney, but from the time she was a teen, she was drawn to the theater. After receiving a law degree, Gewirtz practiced entertainment law.

However, after her first daughter was born, she switched to law school administration, serving as an admissions and career counselor, and then creating and directing a program to assist attorneys with their reentry to law practice or an alternative legal career. Yet, the theater bug started to bite again when her younger daughter, a musical theater actor, began performing with a community theater. While loving her job, Gewirtz was also starting to burn out.

Thinking that she might want to be a Broadway producer, she gave six months' notice at work. While still at her job, she invested in her first Broadway show and took some general commercial theater producing classes to see if this was what she really wanted to do. After taking almost every class the Commercial Theatre Institute (CTI) offered, she applied, and was accepted, to CTI's 14-week advanced class in commercial producing. In 2017, she cofounded and became executive director of Liquid Theatre Collective, Inc., a not-for-profit theater company. Says Gewirtz, "I've been really lucky to have enjoyed each of my career chapters. It has made my life more interesting, I believe, to have had a second and now a third career."

There's power in partnership is the thinking of Betsy Polk and Maggie Ellis Chotas, both age 53. By working together, enjoying what they do, and relishing their camaraderie, these leaders have tackled the challenge of being solitary by making sure someone has their back if there is a health issue or family problem. Polk and Chotas, the co-presidents of The Mulberry Partners, an executive and leadership coaching and consulting firm based in North Carolina, are strong advocates of women working and leading together to achieve better results. They address this in a book they coauthored, *Power through Partnership: How Women Lead Better Together*.

New Yorker Barbara Saidel, 68, gave up a successful career as chief information officer at a top executive search firm and later as chief operating officer of a major nonprofit organization to become a certified Pilates instructor in her post-retirement life. "I've always been a totally type-A person, dedicated to my career, and to my family. I worked 50-to-60-hour work weeks and traveled a great deal on business. I threw myself 150 percent into everything I did. Like other career women of my generation, I always needed to be outstanding," she says.

By the summer of 2008, she realized that she needed a change from the corporate world. "I knew it was time to move on," she says. She volunteered for Obama's presidential campaign and helped design software to fill hundreds of jobs in his administration after he won. The work proved exhilarating and solidified her desire to leave the private sector for a nonprofit job. In late 2010, she accepted the chief operating officer (COO) job for a major religious organization in New York City and worked there for almost seven years. Again, she worked long hours with "complete dedication to the organization," she says. Despite it being a nonprofit, nothing—the hours or the intensity with which she approached her work—had changed "because of who I am," she says.

Then she recognized that she had developed some physical symptoms related to extreme stress. It was time for a more significant step away from that work. Because of an interest she had developed in Pilates, she devoted more time to working out. However, she realized that to continue to improve her Pilates expertise, she needed to practice more often and take private training in addition to participating in classes. It made sense to become a certified instructor. That required 500 hours of training and apprenticeship. Turning 65, the arrival of her first grandchild, and continued concern about her stress spurred more debate about retirement sooner rather than later. She and her husband, a college professor and author, met with their financial advisor to weigh possibilities. Retirement was feasible with lifestyle changes and reduced annual expenses they were willing to make.

With her certification in place, Saidel began teaching at a small New York City studio. "I earn little but love it—the clients I meet and help. And it's good for me, too. We're all building flexibility, balance, and our core strength. My life has become a mosaic of balancing different interests that I love, and which have great meaning. Life is different but very good," she says.

There are those like Chicagoan Judi Schindler, 78, who started a new career far afield of her previous work that brought her back to one of her first loves—acting. "I always wanted to pursue that but knew I could have a better, steadier career as a journalist," she says. For more than 40 years, she worked in public relations, but began winding down in her 60s after she merged her business with someone younger. "I wondered how long I could sustain my business—the overhead, bringing in new clients, buying new directories with lists of companies," she says. She began to imagine a retirement with acting as her main pursuit, so she took classes and signed with an agent. Her first role was a stretch—a white Jewish woman playing a Latina woman, yet she surprised herself with her success. More roles followed, though she found she had to work hard to memorize lines. "I have to work 10 times harder at it than someone in their 20s," she says.

At age 75, she retired, took more classes, performed in more plays, and did voice-over work, film, and commercials. She also wrote a book about husbands because she had so much good comedic material, she says—long before *The Marvelous Mrs. Maisel* became a TV hit. She self-published the book, *Husbands: An Owner's Manual, How to Survive a 50-Year Marriage,* because she wanted to be sure it came out in hard cover and in color. It's both on Amazon and her website, www. judischindler.com.

Unlike her paid work, her second career has cost her money—"a lot," she says, but she sees only the upside. "It's kept me off the streets, I make enough to say I'm a professional actor but not enough to quit my day job (if I had one). I've also had a ball," she says. She also learned one major lesson. "I became far more of a risk taker as I aged, maybe, because I had a financial safety net from my other work," she says. She also had the emotional support of her spouse of 55 years who totally encouraged her decisions.

Susan "Honey" Good, in her 70s, was searching for a new purpose in life and founded an award-winning internet website company, Honeygood.com in 2013, based in Chicago. In 1990 at age 46 she became a widow; her daughters were still in their early 20s. Two years later, she married a real estate executive, and they now have a blended family with 27 grandchildren. During her 60s, she met a professional writer who told her that if she wanted to write, she should keep a journal for three months and never miss a day. "If you do this, I promise you will find your voice," the professional writer said. Good hasn't stopped writing since.

Often labeled as the "cool 21st-century GRANDwoman with Moxie," Good now has 33.8 thousand Instagram followers, authored *Stories for My Grandchild,* and launched a website column in 2020 called "Ask Honey," where she extends a personal helping hand to readers wrestling with all types of situations she herself has experienced: widowhood; moving to Hawaii; blending a second family; surviving two different kinds of cancer; navigating family relationships; family suicide; starting an internet business in her 60s; becoming an author; finding love;

betrayals from other women, as well as confronting agism ("age is just a number"); loneliness; and "invisibility." She answers other kinds of reader questions, too—about beauty, style, decorating, and entertaining, forming women's groups, and traveling the world.

Another project she started in 2020 is a private Facebook group called GRANDwomen with Moxie—"Where Loneliness Disappears"—and podcast. She also wrapped her first internet video commercial for an Easy Spirit Shoes campaign, featuring actress/dancer Debbie Allen.

HOW TO ASSESS
THE CAREER/RETIREMENT LANDSCAPE

No single solution works for all. Certainly, the "old-school retirement" approach of planning for a single day when you leave work for a permanent "vacation" and never return is passé, says Chip Munn, a Florence, South Carolina-based financial advisor, CEO of Signature Wealth, and author of *The Retirement Remix: A Modern Solution to an Old School Problem*. "Most people don't want to do that anymore. Instead, they want to be able to stay active mentally and physically. Old-school retirement is broken because there's no one way to 'do retirement' anymore," he says.

Some of the possibilities work better than others for each person and their spouse/partner if it's not just them. What's needed to get started is a plan, Munn says. Don't procrastinate. It's tempting to defer things that you may want to do now and wait for a later time. "That time may never come," he says. Do what feels right in your gut, put it in the context of your reality, and factor in the following issues, with input from professional advisors, closest loved ones, friends, colleagues, and some who have started to make the change.

Age and health. Because people retire at such different ages, they need to factor in possible longevity. "Someone's retirement could be 20 years or more if they're in their 60s while someone else's could be just five or 10 years," says financial planner Rubin. They may choose to vary how they live over that timetable, but the number of years is significant, she says.

Joseph Hearn, a financial advisor, vice president at Teckmeyer Financial Services LLC in Omaha, Nebraska, and coauthor of *If Something Happens to Me*, suggests factoring in the health and status of your partner or spouse. "If you are in excellent health and have longevity in your family, working a little longer may not significantly cut into your plans. Not so if you or your spouse (partner) are in poor health. In that instance, delaying retirement could mean your chances to do certain things are gone for good. Considering a partner or spouse is particularly true when couples are part of a May-December marriage or relationship," says Hearn.

Although Robert and Edward have a 12-year age gap, Robert says, "We don't think about this, though I must admit that I feel it at times— the more aches and pains I have, the more I think about it." Robert had already retired as a physician to care for a sick wife. Edward was in the process of going back to teaching. "I felt I had a lot to give to the students; I still wanted to play the game." He went to work for the Special School District and a few weeks into the school year, he was diagnosed with an illness. "I took a medical leave from school, spent time recuperating, and decided then to leave teaching to focus on the real estate that I manage part-time," he says.

The fact that Edward works part-time has not interfered with their lives. "I have arranged to be able to do a lot of things how I want to do them and when. I can take off for a month, and I have someone to fill in," Edward says. He likes to work because it keeps him very active rather than watching TV or reading. "I run a little real estate business that makes me use my brain to problem solve and through work I meet many interesting friends. In this respect, work gives me an additional social life and a little pocket change," he adds.

Hearn also suggests on his website, intentionalretirement.com, the idea of a phased retirement or mini retirements. "You could take off six weeks a few times a year or even once," he says. Although he's only 47 and married, Hearn has done this with his wife and worked remotely in different locations, which he explains is different than a vacation. Doing so reflects his advice of not waiting. "It lets me try out the 1.0 version in my 40s, then do a 2.0 version in my 50s, and see what works best or try something else in my 60s," he says.

Partner/spouse. If you're part of a couple, you should be on the same page. Hearn has found that many couples are not in agreement about retirement dreams, plans, and expectations. "One wants to move to the beach and the other wants to stay close to the kids," he says. For financial advisor Rubin that rings true for herself since her spouse is 11 years older and retired a few years ago while she still works full-time.

"It's important to communicate what each feels retirement should look like. We never talked about it until he was ready to, but the conversation could have been started much earlier. In fact, many could start when they marry and then update or change the scenario but at least it's in the open," she says.

This can be an even bigger issue if there's a huge age gap in terms of retirement planning and finances. This is true for Maria, a commercial casting director in her 50s, and her wife of four years, Natalie, 35, who runs a nonprofit pet adoption agency. They admit a big age difference although Natalie is the old soul. The two also own a retail pet store business together in Los Angeles. Neither is ready to even think about retirement and plan to work for years. Says Maria, "I met Natalie when she was in her 20s. We resisted having a relationship for a while because of the age difference. However, we've been together now for 11 years and married for four years. Natalie loves music from the 60s and 70s and old movies . . . and of course, me. We have so much fun together. We basically laugh all day, which is what keeps our relationship strong," she says. They've done little financial planning for the future at this point.

"My 93-year-old mother passed away in October 2019," Maria says. "She had long-term care insurance and I saw what a pain it was. She spent so much money on it and the insurance didn't want to pay for anything. I feel it's not a good plan for me. I'd rather invest my money now and see it grow." They're still working and trying to generate ideas to shore up their finances. "Natalie has her own money and I have mine," says Maria.

"Natalie is more of a spender and I'm more of a saver. It's better if I don't know anything about what she's spending," but she adds, "on one financial point we are on the same page: we feel like we both won the love lottery."

Robert says that regardless of the age difference with Edward, "we really are very compatible and are very happy together. We constantly tell each other how lucky we are to have found each other."

Barbara remembers joking after her divorce that one of the things she and her former husband seemed to disagree about—or so she thought—was where to retire. "I always wanted to go to a place with water. He said he preferred mountains. We had this discussion when spending a weekend in the Berkshire Mountains of Massachusetts. I'm sure we could have worked it out if that was the only problem. Obviously, it wasn't," Barbara says.

Hearn adds, "Make sure you do your planning together so you can work through differences early and enter retirement as a team, even if you're not both retiring at the same time." Even bringing up the subject can be tough for some couples whose communication skills may not be the best. "Try to be flexible about the other's wishes, which may involve each person sacrificing something or agreeing to experiment. It's important to consider my definition of retirement, which involves an intentional way of living based on freedom to follow our pursuits and their choices," he says.

Interests. What gets you excited to get up, get dressed, jump—or crawl—out of bed, and wish you maybe had pursued another career at some juncture? You might not have to chuck your day job but can try out some other work on the side or full-time. Barbara had long planned to become a professional artist, but one journalism course in college piqued her interest, and she landed her first job at a magazine. She used her art history and architecture knowledge to write about a variety of subjects. Almost 11 years ago, she rekindled her interest in painting during a vacation with her family when she took a hike-and-watercolor class. Since then, she has attended paint retreats with other teachers and had a website designed to sell work. She has no plans to stop writing but is having fun painting, which has let her make new friends and see the world through art. "I now look at clouds, mountains, bodies of water, fields, and imagine how I might paint them," she says.

Bucket list. Before retiring, says financial advisor Hearn, everyone should ask themselves: What do I want to do? Where do I want to do it? Who do I want to do it with? Having that information will help give you purpose and plan for how to spend your time. "If your key reason for retiring is to escape your job, wait until you have a plan in place for meaningful pursuits. Doing so will likely help you avoid a bad case of retirement 'buyer's remorse,'" he says. Yet, at the same time, he encourages people not to wait too long. It doesn't give you time if you wait to find out what really makes you happy," he says.

Finances. Even when we have saved, can start to draw Social Security benefits, secure funds from pensions, and have other possible sources of monies to tap, we can never get overconfident. First, few people budget seriously. They may have a loose idea in their heads of what they spend money on and know how much goes out on yearly vacations, daily or weekly lattes, grandkids' gifts, education, and so on, says Rubin. And they should. The reason is simple. It's easier to cut back if you know where money is going, especially if there are big surprise hits such as September 11 and the economic downfall that followed, the financial crisis of 2008/09, the 2020 coronavirus pandemic, and periods of inflation or recession. Owning a home or apartment can mean other hits that are significant, from a new roof to furnace, air conditioner, appliances, and landscaping.

You can always talk to a financial professional at your bank or credit union for help budgeting or drafting a financial retirement plan. Rubin recommends talking with a certified financial planner who adheres to a fiduciary standard of conduct. Interview a few financial professionals and choose one before you retire to develop a budget that you can stick with and adjust when needed. The professional can also keep you accountable and guide you.

There are ways to conserve. "Maybe, you can't give up a latte completely but perhaps keeping it to one a week will help," Rubin says. You don't want to feel you live in a straitjacket but include what's most important to give you joy and cut out what's least important such as that third or fourth cooking magazine subscription. Then there's housing, a big bite of most budgets. An advisor can help decide if it's smart to refinance a mortgage now that interest rates are so low, pay off a mortgage from savings, or downsize to another house, condo, or rent. "Sometimes, going smaller means going nicer so it ends up not being less expensive than staying put and not having to incur moving costs," Rubin says.

Even with Medicare, you will have health expenses, including a monthly fee, along with possible supplemental and drug plan fees. Also, more physicians don't accept insurance so you may have more medical bills unless you work and your employer picks up these expenses. Factor in the costs of eyeglasses, hearing aids, and surgeries that insurance might not cover. Having long-term care insurance, which you may have been funding for years, also adds up and buying it when you're older is tougher and more costly. It may or may not prove worthwhile.

Overall, you are wise to sock away money so you're well protected if you live a long life and can cover unexpected expenses. The rule of thumb is to put aside in savings enough to cover three to six months of essential expenses in case of a problem such as job loss, an illness, or a financial downturn. At the same time, set aside enough for extras that make you happy. An advisor who acts as a fiduciary can help you choose smart balanced investment vehicles that should be right for you. Many investments can be very confusing. Be sure to avoid costly investments offered by people with dubious reputations or lacking expertise. Both of us found advisors who understand our different needs and charge a previously agreed upon fee for managing our investments rather than a commission on each investment made, which raises the red flag of conflict of interest.

We also heed Hearn's advice that smart financial decisions represent more than a math problem. "They permit you to sleep better at night, have a reason to get out of bed in the morning, and add meaning to your life with what you choose to do," he says.

Knowledge. For some, work inspires them to keep learning and sharing after long years in another field, more than they might do on their own, or by reading journals or watching YouTube videos. It lets them fine-tune their skills more rigorously, maybe in gardening, exercise, or personal finance.

Companies can reap the benefits of an aging work force. "I have lots of clients who want to do work inside their career fields because they view it as a way to pass on their wisdom, which I define as information plus experience, to the next generation of leaders," Munn says. "This is a service or even a gift to the team member—future retiree, company, and the next generation. The team member gets to continue to learn and can apply experience to new information. The company and next generation benefit from wisdom that can't be transferred as easily as information," he says. It's akin to serving as a mentor.

Tech skills. If you plan to retire, beef up your technology skills at some point, even if you don't need them for work. You will need them to stay in touch with friends and family. If you don't have a computer, buy one with a camera, along with a printer, headphones perhaps, and microphone for Zoom and Skype meetings online. Or purchase an iPad for video conferencing. Many found these devices invaluable during the 2020 COVID-19 pandemic for staying in touch. Margaret uses the many features in Zoom for virtual tutoring.

Skittish about technology? Hire a computer expert to help set up your tools, teach you skills, and be on call when you need their expertise. Most charge by the hour, and it's a great investment and stress buster, as both of us have found. There's also technology to let them "come in online" remotely to guide you from their home or office, which is not that expensive. You may need updated technology at different points. Barbara has purchased a new hard drive, monitor screen, and new laptop from her expert who is accustomed to her frantic calls. "I can't find the document! Can you help immediately?" Margaret found a new computer expert when she relocated to New York City. He helps her resolve problems by entering her computer remotely. Having your own expert will work better than depending on a different "geek squad" member from a store each time you cry: "help." The person can tailor tech tools to your work, patience level, and budget.

You might also consider hiring a high school or college student to help update skills. They often like earning extra money and may be more patient than your grown children. Barbara did so and asked the young woman to come to her office once a week for an hour. "It was a good time frame to absorb new technology," Barbara says, who became more proficient with texting and posting photos. She recently advised an older friend to do so to keep up with her grandkids in different cities.

Energy/enthusiasm level. It takes effort to get up and get going as we age whether it's the same career or something new. By our mid-to-late 60s and 70s, some want to sleep later, have a leisurely breakfast, come home earlier from work, take a power nap, have dinner, crawl into bed, and do nothing except watch TV or read. However, even reading can be more than we can handle some nights. Most experts advise doing what you can and not pressuring or guilting yourself. It's great to take on a challenge but not overload yourself and burn out. A key, Munn says, is to have passion for what you do. "Spending your days doing things that you want to do rather than things you have to do can lead to years of productive, fulfilling work," he says.

Social company. Some like having a place to get away from their house and be with other people. It's different than just talking on the phone, doing FaceTime, video conferencing, or texting. They may savor sharing ideas face-to-face for the continuous exchange, akin to working as part of a team. They may feel they're just not as good doing this on their own. Both of us loved the daily interaction when we sat side-by-side in Margaret's basement working on our first book. When Barbara moved, a method was in place that could be maintained, thanks to emails, phone calls, and later texting. It wasn't as much fun. For one,

Barbara didn't have access to the same stash of junk food that Margaret kept in her kitchen. Oh, those Oreo cookies and Cheez-It crackers. **Flexibility.** As we've seen with some of our doctor, lawyer, and accountant friends who are still viewed as invaluable by their hospitals, firms, and companies, their employers may allow them to pare back to an agreed upon number of hours rather than step away completely. They still make some money but get to balance the work-play plan better. One doctor we know has given up one week each month and spends time at his country house. Barbara has one friend who's retired but occasionally will "pick" up small jobs to pay for extras such as nice restaurant meals. Margaret's brother-in-law, a retired attorney, still works for a few clients.

Questions to ask yourself to help you decide:

1. How long have you worked and what have you loved/liked and disliked about your job? What might have changed?
2. What is making you think about retiring (be specific)?
3. Have you been a good saver and have enough to live on for years to come in the style to which you've become accustomed?
4. Can you describe your feelings as the date to make a change approaches, if you've made the decision to step away.
5. What will you start to do to make it work if you haven't yet done so? Budget? Cut back on expenses? Downsize? Look for part-time work?
6. Have you consulted experts such as a financial professional, your spouse/partner, grown kids, or friends to glean all facts and possibilities?
7. What do you imagine the first Monday or Tuesday will be like after you retire, change fields, or go part-time?
8. What's your routine now like and what might you miss most that you can still include—people, paycheck, stimulation?
9. Are you thinking about taking on new work to fill in the gap of a paycheck or social interaction?
10. Have you started to take Social Security, or when will you?
11. If your spouse or partner will retire after you, how will that impact your choice? Or, have they already done so and how does that affect your decisions?
12. When you ponder this choice, do you wish you had retired earlier?

Reasons that suggest it may be time to step away:

We've pondered these, too, and why we might choose to step away if all the stars aligned, including winning the lottery or a MacArthur Fellowship "Genius Grant." Then we'd each do something more to help others.

1. Long hours that can't be adjusted and would make it difficult to start enjoying retirement with travel and family.
2. A difficult boss or bosses you never enjoyed working with; ditto for a difficult colleague or colleagues who sabotage work, gossip, or just don't come in on time.
3. Not enough pay for the time and necessary workload at this stage in your life.
4. New and compelling interests that take up a huge chunk of your time. Or, perhaps you're the caregiver for your aging parent and are needed 24/7.
5. Changing technology that takes too long to ramp up and learn.
6. Dread of each workweek.
7. Physical or mental challenges that now make work harder such as problems driving, hearing, seeing, walking, and remembering.

The older years can be a time of leisure and joy. You are freer to explore new options, give up all or some of your work, or retire to something new you enjoy rather than retire from something to nothing. Or, you can continue working. There's no one solution. You get to decide.

Chapter Nine

Joy to Our World

Time to Focus on Our Passions

When Margaret's husband retired after 42 years of work in two industries and four main jobs, he looked for things to do. There was only so much golf he could play, walks he could take with their dog, or times he could mow their lawn. One day Margaret found him matching socks in his sock drawer and another time polishing leaves on plants. They laughed. He knew it was time to find something more substantive to do with his energy and time.

He debated. When Margaret asked him, "What do you really want to do?" a kind of whirring emptiness flapped in front of his eyes. He couldn't imagine that he might have an innumerable number of choices at age 61. Margaret reminded him how much he loved jazz. He had been a child musician who loved playing the drums and had wanted to become a professional jazz musician as an adult. His parents nixed the idea, telling him he needed a job with steady income, like his father who worked as a pharmacist. She soon saw the gleam of an idea in his eye.

The next day he approached a local jazz station to ask if he could work for it. With his vast knowledge of jazz and ability to talk to anyone about almost anything, as well as knowing how to sell almost anything to anybody, the station hired him on the spot to sell ads. The promise was that he could do some on-air work. It was the happiest Margaret had seen him in years. He worked there for a few years until a more challenging offer came along to do work for a movie advertising company.

We work, structure our lives around our jobs and family members, attempt to balance the demands of each, put money into retirement accounts, pay off mortgages, and try to keep up our healthful habits, and preventive medical steps. The list continues. Then we may start new careers or hobbies we've long wanted to pursue.

The bottom line is that we reach a time when it's good to pay ourselves back for our years of hard work and do what we wished we had had more time for. At last, it's our turn to play.

That's what a friend, "Ruth," in her late 50s, learned. She worked for a financial services firm planning events. Her children had left her nest years before and her husband had died. One morning she walked into work and spotted a pink slip on her desk. Instead of bemoaning the fact that she was laid off, she decided it was the opportune time to retire and do all the things she never had time for yet had a passion for such as shopping, lunches with friends, happy hours, traveling, and trying her hand at painting. She signed up for art classes and made plans to travel abroad for several weeks. Next in the works might be a consulting business.

A passion is something that makes you glow and feel alive. When engaged in your passion—whether a game of poker, gardening, baseball, wine collecting, or anything enjoyable that requires focus, it blocks out the rest of the world. Stress dissolves. You're less cranky, more at peace, and probably smiling more often, which is important to do while you still have teeth. Some turn their passion into a second career as Margaret's husband did.

And then there's Reverend Georgiette Morgan-Thomas, who goes by the name, "The Rev." At age 71, and after being a cancer survivor, she grew a business, American Hats LLC in Philadelphia, all from her passion for hats. At one time, she owned more than 100 hats and had converted a bedroom in her home into a closet to store them. When she heard that the hat factory she loved was being shuttered four years ago, she bought it with her life savings. She brought in her son who had attended law school to handle the books and other administrative tasks. Nine months after the purchase, the wholesaler they had worked with who featured their hats in catalogues took its hat business to China. American Hats had to create a new base.

Her staff began to make hats with no trim and then market them to individual designers to decorate them. It became a big thing for young people to buy the untrimmed hats. Seeing a niche for plain felt and straw hats, the firm shifted focus to that and opened a showroom in

Harlem, New York. "Then Google came calling. They did a film on my company and selected us as a small business to grow with Google. This meant they'd share all digital tools, which gave us an online presence," says The Rev.

A year later, the company was given the opportunity as one of 83 small businesses to apply for space in the Philadelphia Fashion District Mall to be part of Uniquely Philly, a curated space dedicated to growing and supporting Philly's small businesses. "The judges viewed the Google film online and were very impressed with our social media presence," said the Rev. With a highly visible retail space and millions in foot traffic, it was a breakthrough moment. Heading toward $500,000 in sales in 2020, the coronavirus pandemic interrupted its growth. "When the coronavirus pandemic subsides, we will hit the ground running, beat this thing, and reach the $1 million mark."

Sometimes, it takes a while to discover a passion. And often it comes after putting off a long list of excuses—no time or money, questionable talent, no idea how to start, fear of failure. Sometimes, the efforts don't work out as envisioned. Marti Stricker, 66, retired from her job as an accounting clerk for a nonprofit at age 61. Her husband had already retired from his job. "We have no children, are tight with a buck, and saved hoping to retire early," she says.

Initially, Stricker used her new free time to catch up on long-planned house projects, start on her bucket list, and explore multiple volunteer opportunities, including as a grade-school tutor. However, those hopes were sidetracked when she found herself more involved in the day-to-day care of her mother, who died at 97 after spending more than three years in an assisted living facility. Her brother, who shared responsibilities, died a year and a half before their mother did, leaving sole responsibility to her. She says, "Like Caroline Kennedy Schlossberg, I now have no immediate family left," though she does have nieces and nephews who live close.

After putting her mother in assisted living and starting to declutter the house to eventually sell it, Stricker says, "That's when it hit me that my husband and I had all this clutter too. We don't want to leave this mess for anyone so we're in the process of organizing and getting rid of what we don't need." This is using up a huge chunk of Stricker's time right now, and at some point, she wants to get back to one of her passions, which is volunteering.

Some may begin a passion or hobby after they keep coming back to the idea, stop procrastinating, and decide, why not now? It could start in an unexpected way. You may get involved with a political candidate or write a letter to a Congressional representative to let them know where you stand and to encourage them to consider your position. That might take research and then lead to lots of follow-up. The work gets done and you realize, "Hey, I'm pretty good at this, let's try another cause." It can translate into standing up in a town meeting or even before your condo or co-op board and voicing your opinion or running for local office.

Perhaps, you read an article online about do-gooders saving a rain forest and think, "I can do that or at least learn more about it. And I've always wanted to go to South America." You hear something on a TV cooking show about how to make a delicious yet simple meat stew and broccoli rabe salad and this leads you on a cooking jag. You're walking down a city street and spot someone homeless, and it sparks a conversation about how terrible the problem is. You care about Black Lives Matter, hear about a class on racism, and think, as Margaret did, "I'll sign up. It's time I learned more about white privilege." Or, you're talking to friends and family about what adds joy in their spare time. One says, "playing golf" and the other says "napping." Ding. Ding. When something triggers your interest you think, "I'd like to try that." For years Barbara had tucked aside the idea about taking a class on her religion, and then she did when there was an opening.

An article by food writer Kim Severson in the *New York Times* profiled Dolester Miles of the Highlands Bar and Grill in Birmingham, Alabama, who the James Beard Foundation named outstanding pastry chef of the year. Impressive, but even more so because she taught herself to bake and worked at the prestigious restaurant for years. Her talent for preparing classic Southern cakes and pies whet the appetite of many and maybe spurred some to consider picking up a whisk, spatula, cake pan, or pie plate.[1]

After watching a pie-making episode on the food channel, Margaret decided to try to make a perfect, homemade crust, something she had never done. She took a class at a local cooking school. It proved fun and edifying. She proceeded to crank out pie after pie at home filled with peaches, cherries, and chocolate cream. The effort became a short-lived passion as her attempts at making the crust literally crumbled. Undeterred, she went back to baking her favorite chocolate chip cookies, gingerbread men, and lemon bars, but extended her repertoire after Barbara gifted her Dorie Greenspan's *Dorie's Cookies*. Soon, she finessed the recipes for snowy-topped brownie drop (chocolate crinkle) cookies, Princeton gingersnaps, rosemary-parm cookies, Ms. Corbitt's pecan cake fingers, and tart lemon cookies.

Debby Gaal, 70, a mutual friend of Barbara and Margaret, who now lives in Southern California, always adored theater. "As much as I wanted to pursue it as a career, I was too timid to declare I deserved that path. I fell victim to the belief I wasn't good enough, as well as pressure from my family to stick to a solidly traditional journey: marriage, children, business, practicality. I was a good girl, a pleaser. So, I convinced myself that so many people were more talented than me, I had no right to declare such a frivolous pursuit. While that may have been accurate, it didn't address my ache for the theater world I would leave behind. But creativity never leaves us. If it's not nurtured, it doesn't blame us, it simply lies dormant, patiently, with no time constraints, until we slow down enough to make space in our psyche to nurture our muses."

Fast-forward decades. She says, "My second marriage to the right partner and financial stability (blessings I don't take lightly) has given me the opportunity to do and be anything. In the space of thinking about what that might be, my muses came to life and gave me stories (my new story in writing). I published my first book, *The Dream Stitcher*. I love creating characters and escaping into someone else's world. And I've discovered that other people resonate with what I've created and find joy and meaning in it. Finding readers in that juncture has fueled me to keep writing. A bonus: the most fun I've had in this 20-year pursuit of story has been the recording of the audiobook from Verity Audio Productions in 2020. I'm acting again, something I never thought possible. The hole in my heart has finally healed. I conquered my demons of loss and inadequacy. I feel brave." She also says, "I am grateful for my journey. I recognize that I would not be able to create art without those years of working, motherhood, and personal upheaval."

TIME TO TAKE ADVANTAGE OF TIME

As we get older and step back from work on a full- or part-time basis, we generally have more time to pursue interests. Even if you're not retired, there is a world of choices to test the waters and try to enrich your life, which might prove helpful for long-term commitments. Know too that if you start one or two possible pursuits and they don't prove satisfying or you feel like a failure when you miss every ball in tennis and learn that love in this sport isn't what you thought it was, you don't need to keep going. Stop, reassess, or move forward. As Doris M. Smith, American author of award-winning children's books, said, "I haven't failed at anything, I've just found all the wrong ways of doing it." Use the time with joy rather than waste it and be frustrated.

- **Take classes.** Learn a new language, take a lifelong learning course for seniors, try Pilates and yoga, work with a trainer, learn glassblowing or sculpting, take acting lessons, join a theater group or chorus. Dying to learn more about wine? Visit wineries and go to tastings, even at your local wine and liquor store. Still not sure? Read the newspaper or magazines, listen to podcasts, pay attention to what folks do in articles or on TV shows. The chef on the TV series *Delicious* probably inspired many; same goes for all those female detectives on British whodunits.
- **Make a list of books you want to read or reread.** If you have children, consider the books that they read in high school or college. Why not a self-tutorial on Jane Austen or Charles Dickens? Too old school? Consider all those hilariously funny Nora Ephron, Martin Amis, or David Sedaris books. Or join a local book club, maybe through your library for lively discussions. Peruse bookstores, for many offer staff recommendations.
- **Trace your roots.** Study genealogy. Dig deep and find out who you are because of where you came from. Take an AncestryDNA test. After a while, the search can become an addiction. A first cousin of Margaret's has become almost obsessive pursuing her ancestry and moved to Ireland to find her mother's roots. The good news is that today's software makes the hunt easier. Maybe you're related to someone with a very different ethnic background or religion.
- **Learn to cook or ramp up your skills with classes.** Today there are many food blogs online, TV shows, as well as so many interesting new cookbooks for specialty tastes, diets, and health issues—lactose intolerant, gluten-free, veggie, vegan, dessert-obsessed. One friend of Barbara's is in a coed international cooking group and through the

theme of each meal, diners have "gone" to Mexico, Sweden, Peru, and other destinations. Another friend of Barbara's barely cooked; her husband did. She decided she preferred her choice of spices and combinations, took classes at home, and now has a modest repertoire.

- **Set up a consulting business.** This can take all sorts of directions and can relate to what you did in your career or take a different path. Ideas include freelance graphic arts design, technology, music composition, and tutoring those for whom English is a second language. You don't have to get paid if you don't need the income, but you may earn some. Also, because of technology, you can teach the classes online.

- **Take a bow.** You can share knowledge on a sporadic basis. If you're a musician, offer your talent to a local high school (perhaps one of your grandkids attends) and one where the budget has dictated trimming those types of classes. Same goes for art. Advertise your skills on LinkedIn, Facebook, a website you design (perhaps you took a class to learn how to do this), and other sites. You might even learn tweeting to share your talents or become so proficient at social media that you teach others. Who knows? This could lead to a second career or volunteer gig.

- **Develop a new talent or go back to one you dropped earlier in life.** Learn photography, Photoshop, bridge, Mahjong, or writing children's books, as one friend of Barbara's is now doing in private tutorials with an editor. During the 2020 coronavirus pandemic, many took out their sewing machines and became master mask makers, as Margaret's friend Pat in St. Louis did. You always wanted to make and restore furniture. The husband of one of Barbara's friends does that in their garage and another of her friends makes birdhouses. It also may be a time to master something outlandish like how to do a headstand in a yoga class. Margaret used to sing opera and oratorio music and has debated whether to fine-tune her singing chops again. *La, la, la.*

- **Travel.** It's great fun to research and plan an itinerary. In fact, some like that even more than the actual trip. So, many of us tend to make lists of the places we'd like to go—in our heads, on our tablets, and in thin air. There are online resources to help generate ideas. You don't have to go posh but can stay in affordable rentals and exchange houses on several online sites almost for free. Most of Barbara's and

Margaret's friends love to travel while they are relatively healthy. They like walking, climbing hills, and lying on gorgeous, sandy beaches. Or, you can travel to learn and find a new passion along the route. Leslie Scallet Lieberman and her husband, Maury, both of whom are now in their 70s but retired in their 50s, did. They loved to travel internationally together. But after visiting 75 countries, they wanted to do something useful to help with different world problems they witnessed up close. Starting with a trip to the Philippines where they sponsored a few children, they found ways to use their professional experience to become advisors to the sponsoring international organization.

- **Do more of nothing.** There's nobody watching you punch a time clock or report in on where you've been if you take a long 2½-hour lunch, leave early on a Friday, sit on the couch and play video games, or stare at the walls. At last, you're the boss, the big cheese, and you can relax. Feel like reading online, going to a movie or the theater in the afternoon on a weekday, baking at night, listening to NPR in the morning, napping, or even binge-watching TV reruns of *Law and Order*? Now's the time. Do so without guilt. No more rules or a boss's dirty looks.

WAYS TO ENGAGE YOUR MIND AND BODY

1. Take on a project—scrapbook, arrange photos, take videos, hike, explore.
2. Blog on a topic where you're an expert of sorts, then continue to do so on a regular basis.
3. Spend an hour or more with girlfriends schmoozing, gossiping or working out.
4. Attend a morning coffee concert, service at temple, mosque, or church, or community lecture.
5. Take out an aging parent or elderly friend and spend quality time with them, ask them to tell stories of their past, and tape their conversation.
6. Find someone to date if single and interested; and if in a relationship, snuggle before a fire or watch a movie on TV.
7. Get a new hairdo, dress, nails polished a pretty color, or have a facial or massage.

8. Prepare for a family holiday after the 2020 coronavirus pandemic. Gather everyone together first for a new house signature drink and hors d'oeuvres and sit around the table with place cards, flowers, and after-dinner games.
9. Gather friends and consider using a theme, such as a costume party, high school prom, or dance party with disco ball.
10. Call friends or family you haven't talked to recently and check in on how they are.
11. Write an old-fashioned note or send a card with a note. Everybody likes mail that's not a bill.
12. Read a section of a newspaper or article in a magazine you usually skip over and learn something—maybe it's a crossword puzzle or a piece about sports that's usually not part of your wheelhouse.

TAKE A RISK; YOU MIGHT LIKE IT . . . OR NOT!

When was the last time you stepped out of your comfort zone to try something beyond your usual routine? It's so easy to stay with what you've always done, maybe from fear or laziness, or both. Trying the unexpected helps to keep most of us young, engaged, and perhaps exhilarated. It doesn't have to be a lifetime commitment, like Margaret's attempt at pie baking. Barbara flew twice in a date's private plane. She dislikes flying in big commercial jets, so this tested her nerves, though sitting in the copilot's seat felt safe at the time. After the second time when thick yellow pollen filled the sky, she resolved never to do that again. Fortunately, she grounded the relationship as well.

Why do we decide to take a risk? Life coach Margot Schulman shares a series of thought-provoking and heart-opening questions to ask yourself to shift out of fear, resistance and apathy and into a state of excitement, confidence, and courage. Schulman suggests asking yourself these questions and highlighting the ones that make your heart beat faster or your breath catch in your throat to help you figure out your direction and possibilities:

1. If you knew deep in your bones that you could not fail, what would you try or attempt?

2. How would you live your life differently if you knew that you would be accepted, loved, and admired by the people who matter most to you no matter what?
3. What would a normal day in your life look like if you felt 100 percent secure financially, physically, and emotionally?
4. If you had hard scientific proof that you would go to Heaven when you die, no matter how you live the rest of your days, how would you change your life?

Once you have picked one question to focus on (you can also create your own question, using the above as inspiration), give yourself 10 or 15 minutes to write down your answer, she says. When you are finished, look it over and pick one thing to which you can commit. You can also use the question as a template for a supportive daily mantra. For example, if the question that resonated most for you was, *what would a normal day in your life look like if you felt 100 percent secure financially, physically, and emotionally?* you can say to yourself every day while brushing your teeth, *I am 100 percent secure financially, mentally, and emotionally.* It does not matter if you do not believe this to be true at first, just saying it every day—even out loud—will shift your mindset into more confidence and courage to change your pattern and take a leap into new possibilities.

New Yorker Fran Kaufman, 80, started pursuing photography more than 20 years ago. "My father was 54 when he died suddenly on the way to work, and I didn't want that to happen to me. I had an incredibly stressful job. When there was a change in management, it became a good time to leave. I didn't know what to do with all my new time. I had worked since I was 16 years old. I went to the gym, and like most gyms, there was a yenta, or busybody, who seemed to know all about everything. When I discussed my situation, she asked me, 'What are you interested in?' After I said photography, she recommended an evening adult class at The Cooper Union in New York City. It was hard to get in, but I did, and the first class was incredible," she says. "I was nervous about my work—and still am, but I loved what I was doing. I photograph jazz musicians playing, recording, and practicing. I did a blog for a radio station five days a week for eight years. Some of my photos of musicians are in the Library of Congress. I have photographed many jazz festivals, concerts, and street scenes," she says. Kaufman leased a studio and found a mentor with whom she continues to meet online. The passion, she says, has added meaning, fulfillment, and purpose to her life. "It allows me to spend what's left of my life indulging myself." Most recently she's photographing patients with dementia.

There are many other options. You might try a new ritual to observe a holiday or volunteer for a project you knew little to nothing about but which you hoped would help others. It certainly doesn't have to involve going away or spending big bucks. It may be for free. Then evaluate. Did it feel good or uncomfortable in the beginning? Was it a disappointment or a way to celebrate that you could venture afield? No one is grading you. This is supposed to be for fun. If Plan A doesn't work out, go for B or C.

Throughout her career as a nonprofit executive and founder of a consulting firm, Margery Leveen Sher, 72, who lives in Washington, DC, had always written articles and spoken on subjects relevant to her work with childcare and work-life balance. While still working full-time in 2012, she decided to start writing about lighter topics, which included a blog titled "Aging Boomer Chick Diatribes" under the pen name Abby Ceedee (for ABCD). About a year later, she looked at her body of work and decided to rebrand and incorporated as "The Did Ya Notice?® Project." She wrote about things she noticed—amazing things, funny things, annoying things.

In 2014, while still working, she self-published *The Noticer's Guide to Living and Laughing*, which incorporated her blog posts. She continued to write and post new noticing posts on other social media outlets.

Once retired in 2016, she began writing full-time and speaking professionally as a "Noticer." She also took on other subjects.

Because of her serious interest in what was happening to immigrants in this country, she penned and self-published in 2020 her most recent book, *Indomitable! Immigrants' Stories of Perseverance and Resilience*.

She has enjoyed being able to write. "Writing has always been my passion, but once I gave up my paycheck (I never say I am retired), I could devote myself fully to writing projects and speaking. I take a break from all the writing by holding volunteer jobs, tutoring, and teaching adult immigrants—hence the impetus for my book *Indomitable*," she says.

The writing has also brought positive feedback, which adds greater personal pleasure. "My favorite comment from the work on noticing has been, 'You are the greatest therapist.'"

Ideas to test a passion:

1. Give most new efforts at least two or three tries, whether it's tennis, knitting, sailing, bicycling, or scuba diving. When it becomes a drag, time to move on. Treat it like a blind date or bad relationship.
2. If it appeals, stay with it longer and set some goals. Try a 10-mile bicycle ride, joining a bike group, or ordering some new biking outfits after your 20-mile ride. Go up bigger hills or plan a bike vacation.
3. Change it up so it doesn't become stale. If you've taken up cooking, try a new approach to an old recipe (i.e., make your chocolate chip cookies by using brown butter or sprinkling sea salt atop when they are warm). Cook with a friend who's great at dim sum and teaches you how to prepare the filling, stuff wrappers, and sauté them.
4. Journal about your new passion, which helps you assess what you like about it—or don't. You may find that journaling ironically becomes a new passion.
5. Mix it up. Instead of an exercise class with several folks where you go left when the instructor says go right, try a private session if it's affordable. That's what Margaret chose when she started Pilates, as did Barbara.
6. Limit the number of passions you pursue simultaneously. One at a time lets you focus.
7. Keep in mind that nothing must be forever. You can stop and remember your passion as something you enjoyed—or not. Maybe singing is not your thing. Better to end anything on a high C-note.

DO GOOD, FOR IT DOES
GOOD FOR YOU AND THE WORLD BEYOND

Passions can also be do-good deeds for others and take the focus off you. The opportunities are limitless. As baby boomers, we envision these years as an extraordinary opportunity to make a difference not just by writing checks but by rolling up our sleeves and digging in with action and words to help those less well-off physically, mentally, and financially. No single approach works when it comes to volunteer opportunities, except that it must be something you'll enjoy rather than dread. We think the recipients in need make up a very long list: our country, states, cities, villages, towns, parks, healthcare, educational systems, the older population—often isolated and lonely—and the younger population—often with few resources and little family, and sometimes with little hope.

What you can do varies widely. Some like to mentor, tutor, and work with youths. Others enjoy office work, teaching art or crafts, running events, stewarding, entertaining, and coaching older folks. Many we know like to sit on nonprofit boards because they have strong administrative skills and like the camaraderie.

A friend of ours volunteers to coach soccer for inner-city kids. A relative spends one day a week volunteering to work with seniors, reading to them, fixing something that's broken in their homes, or serving as a companion, so they don't feel so alone. Others we know drive seniors to appointments since they may not have transportation. Margaret has two friends who work in food pantries. Another friend of hers who loves dogs and has golden retrievers does pet therapy in hospitals and nursing homes. A man we know takes kids on missions through his church to build houses for underserved folks.

Frequently, volunteering can be related to work we once did but can now do in a pro-bono way. Scallet an attorney and nonprofit executive, had worked on mental health and broader health problems. Her husband Maury had overseen programs on program planning, prevention, and workplace issues at a national mental health agency. Both were able to leave their jobs and, after surviving some scary medical issues, felt that life was too short not to shift gears. They applied their knowledge and energy to social problems they cared about. They pursued opportunities for unpaid consulting work with organization leaders and also served on nonprofit boards and committees. They found they enjoyed working in tandem. For example, Maury was a board member and later board chair for a suicide prevention group and recruited Scallet to serve as an advisor on organizational and advocacy issues, which is among her areas of expertise. Together, they catapulted the group to become the leading advocacy voice for suicide prevention in Congress. They led the move to fold their advocacy group into the largest nonprofit in the field.

They also found opportunities to explore individual interests. Scallet became a member of a board on history education. "This was a deep longtime interest of mine. I had long wondered about the 'path not taken' in my own life, which would have been teaching history at some level," she says.

Today, Scallet says, their objectives have evolved toward providing advisory and financial support for people who are working on important social problems. "We look for projects that provide immediate impact but also can have long-term influence." As the two look to the future, they are working with several universities and arts organizations to develop programs, then support implementation with substantial charitable gifts. Scallet stresses that "we look for ideas that will encourage communities and especially young people to be active participants in advancing an equal and inclusive society."

We both believe one person can make a difference and that nothing feels as good as doing good. It can lower the risk of depression because you help others and have strong social interactions. It can give you a sense of purpose and fulfillment, keep you mentally and physically active, which increases brain function, and can reduce stress levels and blood pressure. It can also calm you and lead to a feeling of great joy. It's like the feeling when your endorphins kick in during rigorous exercise because of a release of dopamine in the brain. Also, by doing good, you likely gain the opportunity to change yourself and leave a legacy.

With age and insight comes the important lesson that a legacy isn't about having a statue built in your honor or your name placed in a big font on a hospital, university, or museum building, as the main character in the TV show *Billions* did. And it's also not about having a long (expensive) obituary placed in a newspaper or epitaph written on your gravestone.

Rather, according to Rabbi Moses ben Maimon (or Maimonides), a person's legacy is much more connected to an eight-step methodology known as Rambam's ladder. Maimonides was a pillar of Jewish scholarship who lived under Muslim rule in the 12th century and is also known by the nickname Rambam. The ladder ranks levels of *tzedakah* based on compassion and common sense. *Tzedakah,* a term often translated to mean charity, is in fact much more closely tied to justice, explains Lisa Lisser, a New York teacher of Jewish wisdom. Based on this principle, the most meaningful way to give, and the highest level of Rambam's ladder, is to create a business partnership with a person who needs a livelihood. To strengthen the hand of the poor, you must teach them a trade. The ultimate act of *tzedakah* is to give in a way that doesn't embarrass or shame the recipient.

The second-highest level of giving requires anonymity on the part of both the benefactor and the recipient. This highlights the goal that giving *tzedakah* is incumbent on all of us, not simply a way to make a name for ourselves.

Knowing you have the power, resources, and commitment to give not only benefits others, but also gives you a reason to look forward to every day, says Lisser, still in her 50s. She gave up her work as an attorney to rediscover her Judaism and share her knowledge with students of all ages. Her preferred legacy is to make a difference in someone's life by opening their eyes and hearts to life lessons that may have been hidden in Jewish tradition.

No matter where our days take us, we believe in finding joy by living more in the moment and treasuring those times. It's up to us to do what we wish without pressure or guilt from ourselves or others. Throughout our adult lives, we often found ourselves in stressful roles. No more encores for those parts. Today, we want to live our lives in happily ever afters.

Chapter Ten

Social Capital

How to Stay Connected While Single and Aging

As we age, our social capital—the connections we have with others that build trust and support—shifts like a supply and demand curve. If we are retired, there is reduced contact with former work colleagues. The deaths of friends and family members or loved ones moving away means social capital with them is on the wane or gone.

There's a truism that we both sadly found to be accurate based on our experiences. If you lose your spouse to death or divorce, your social capital may decline or change. Both divorce and widowhood spotlight the fact that this world is made for twosomes. We can probably blame it on Noah, who told the animal kingdom to send two of each kind to his ark.

We sadly learned firsthand from Margaret about widowhood, and how someone is wined, dined, and included in social events for roughly a year. Friends and family almost take pity on you and try to help you heal by getting you out of the house if you've been hiding there unable to function. Widows are at a low point shortly after losing their spouses. At the time a widow is grieving, they are negotiating new social territory with female and couple friends. Some men, we've heard, might try to seduce them, thinking they're lonely, vulnerable, missing intimacy, and willing to get close to any semblance of a guy. Our advice: don't. Gossip spreads faster than the coronavirus pandemic of 2020 did.

There is no timetable in this uncharted territory for grieving, maybe finding a new mate, or making new friends. You may shut down and resign yourself to being alone or only socializing with like-minded and like-status singles. Or, if you miss being with your former couple friends, you recognize that it's no one's job but your own to pull yourself up and rejoin polite society.

As two women, one of whom was widowed and the other divorced, we had to figure out how to rebuild our social capital in the new context of our lives. Being divorced can be different than being widowed, Barbara learned. You're often cut out of the social world sooner as former couple friends become as distant as a remote tropical island. Some may view you as competition, looking to snare their husband or partner; others view your status as contagious. Being around you may lead to a closer examination of their own marriage and its failures. Still others won't like the logistics of an odd number around the dining table, so don't expect an invite until you have a plus-one to include. Then, you might be sought out since so many will be inquisitive about who you're with. "What's he like?" they wonder.

Also, whether you're divorced or widowed, many couples don't want to deal with the annoying question of how to divide the check for your portion if you were included at a restaurant meal. Not all, but some want you to pick up your tab, but they also feel that makes them look cheap if they allow you to do so. At the end of the day, many couples find that it's simpler for the wife to include you at an all-gals' meal mid-week. That also eases their guilt. Don't take it personally. Yet, of course, it's personal. You know you're good company, but your new single status upsets the social balance.

Barbara, who was divorced from her husband after 31 years, likes to socialize with couples. She missed the male energy and prefers mixed company gatherings. That doesn't preclude her enjoyment of her gals-only events, but she likes a balance. Margaret, a widow, enjoyed being part of a couple again two years after her husband died. Now again on her own, she loves spending time with couple friends but enjoys even more the time spent with her girlfriends in a group or with guy friends, one on one. Perhaps that's because she was married for 42 years and devoted most of that time to her husband, kids, and their couple friends. She had less gal- or guy-only time.

Regardless of why your social capital has changed, if you're in the loss column on a balance sheet, you can reinvest in new relationships and try to build up your portfolio. Ironically, most of us will be alone at some point, we just don't know when and how it will feel until it happens. However, we know that the loss of social contacts can have a direct impact on our mental and physical well-being. There is no pill to take to make you feel better. It takes diligent social strategizing.

With so much discussion about the negative consequences of isolation in our lives—lack of human touch, fewer face-to-face conversations, less fun, joy, aloneness, loneliness, more anxiety, physical illnesses, and depression, it's no wonder that we worry about how to stay connected once we're no longer connected. In Denworth's book, *Friendship,* she writes that social integration and connection feature prominently in areas where people live to be 100 or more.[1] She quotes others, including psychologist and author Susan Pinker, who wrote in her book, *The Village Effect: Why Face-to-Face Contact Is Good for Our Health, Happiness, Learning, and Longevity,* that geographic proximity to close friends and family is what matters more than numbers. The good news is that it doesn't have to take a village—though in some cases it might to form some strong bonds.[2]

For most of our adult lives, since we each married at age 22, we never worried about being on our own and how we would spend our nights and weekends. We were with these men and a good-size group of friends most weekends. We were courted socially and included, and we included others. We may even have become complacent about marriage as a permanent union. Some we knew clung to their marriages despite less than stellar relationships, particularly in later years. It was easier to ignore annoying habits and behavior and carve out alone time rather than divorce and start over. Divorce is terrible on many levels, especially on most women's financial net worth unless they were the big bread earner or from a wealthy family.

When we each found ourselves on our own, we had a huge learning curve of what to do with all our newfound time and how to stay connected socially. Barbara had long included singles, women and men, following her mother's example, who never thought of people as only worthy if they arrived in pairs. Barbara realized that if she wanted to be included post-divorce, she'd have to extend invitations and reciprocate. And so, she did—to her home for dinner since she liked to cook and to restaurants, picking up the tab by usually slipping a maître d' or waiter her credit card or cash like a secret handshake. One couple regularly invited her to the retirement house they had built on a lake. The wife even told her, with the husband's approval, "You can spend as much time here as you want." They annually included her for a New Year's Eve weekend, a dreaded milestone for many singles in the beginning.

Not all friends were as generous. A few shunned her. One couple never invited her over or out to eat but at the time of her younger daughter's wedding the wife was miffed that they hadn't been included when they barely knew that daughter. She stopped communicating with Barbara. Others invited her a few times, then cut her off. Had Barbara said something wrong? Not said "thank you" enough?

She knew not to drone on about her protracted divorce and say anything negative about her former husband. Nobody really cared after the initial burst of inquisitiveness about what had transpired, she found. In fact, one acquaintance bluntly reminded her of the protocol after Barbara said something about the divorce in a passing conversation. "You've talked about this enough," the person said. Her reprimand silenced Barbara. In most cases, Barbara's reaction was not bitterness but acceptance that these people were insensitive to what singlehood was like.

When Barbara moved years later to a village with one main stoplight in Upstate New York, where she knew nobody, she found that many didn't care if she was single. They were more interested in what she did in her work and free time, whose house she had bought, why she had relocated from the Midwest, and how she planned to help improve village life. It reminded her of fictional Stars Hollow in Connecticut from the TV series *Gilmore Girls* where single mother Lorelai Gilmore raised her daughter. All the quirky characters, many single, were judged more by their personality, talents, and kindness to others.

Margaret faced similar challenges. A year after her husband's death, invitations started to slow, except for those from her closest circle. One couple continued to include her in monthly restaurant dinners, and another always had her to holiday and New Year's Eve celebrations. Other couples would include her periodically in their weekend plans. At the same time, people would say, "We're going to call to make a date." Many never did. Another friend suggested getting together when they thought she was still dating someone. When Margaret explained they had broken up, the friend suggested the two gals have lunch.

Though Margaret and her late husband hadn't entertained very much, she started to do so to pay back those who had been generous to her. She also invited new friends, both couples and singles, she had made.

She found she loved it and was good at it with input from one sister who guided her about setting the table and arranging a floral centerpiece. Margaret took out the good dishes. She knew to open her good wine and liquor. She studied online recipes and experimented in advance. Once she moved to New York City, she was ready to repeat her repertoire with a new circle.

"Priscilla," a 72-year-old who lives in a suburb outside a large Eastern city, found 99 percent of couple friends didn't include her after each of her two marriages ended in divorce. Weekend invites from those who had vacation homes stopped entirely. Some of the women met her for lunch. This was all despite her asking to be included. "It doesn't seem to make a difference. I wonder if they see me as a 'loose atomic particle' that might cause instability in the established order and balance of things? Or, perhaps, I'm just a reminder of the unthinkable—divorce or death. Maybe it has to do with the person's generosity of spirit or lack thereof. Perhaps, it's nothing as profound as all that? It's difficult, however, because it's an additional loss that hurts on top of the primary loss and at a time when you need companionship and support more," she says.

Instead of trying to spur togetherness by asking couples or singles out or having them to dinner, she became paralyzed, felt sorry for herself, and made other plans. After so many excluded her, she decided she didn't want to see them anyway because she had bad feelings. She pursued her many interests, met up with female friends, and started dating and traveling on her own.

What we each found we missed most as singles—and which many others find, too, as they age and are on their own—isn't the food, wine, restaurants, or getting dressed up. It's the shared conversations, storytelling, laughs, hugs, handshakes, smiles, and the repartee back and forth. On our own, we each have plenty of deafening silence. With others we want noise. And we want the kind not just with women, but also with the deep, baritone voices filled with male energy, different conversations, and points of view. In many cases, the men had been our friends. Leaving them out was one more loss.

Rather than feel slighted, we moved on. We needed to make ourselves happy, learn to live authentic lives, reinvent ourselves for singlehood, and make new social and couple friends who welcomed us and gave us a fresh window on life and togetherness. We consulted relationship experts, therapists, authors, friends, and even clairvoyants to ask how we might do so. We found that we weren't doing such a bad job by trusting our gut and adjusting to our new roles.

"Regina," 74, faced being single twice—first after a divorce when she was in her 50s and second after she remarried a physician from another country. "I think my experience having lived in a marriage for a long time and then finding myself a single woman does not differ much from other women in the same situations around the world," she says.

After her first 20-year marriage ended, it left a void, she says, but she was busy in her work and in good financial shape. Her social situation changed, however. She had a circle of friends, one of whom was her bestie for many years who included her every time she had a party with people outside their group of friends. "I was mostly the only single woman among married couples but that was okay for me. Otherwise the phone stopped ringing. Friends and acquaintances disappeared, or I was not invited to parties. If invited to a large celebration, I was placed at the table's end."

She was divorced for seven years before meeting her second husband, several years older. They had an extensive social life, mostly a mix of married people. His friends became her friends, and her friends became his, and they each made new friends in their small Italian village where they owned a country house. When he died in 2018, she moved back to her native country at age 72 to find that her circle of friends was still there but not as close as they used to be. She was once again a single woman and relegated to "lunches with the girls," she says.

Disappointingly, her best friend, who had been her pillar after her divorce, was no longer there as "best friend." She was in a new relationship. "I had my family—two children, their spouses, and four grandchildren, and I still met my old group of girlfriends. I had some acquaintances, but no real close friends, and I felt rather lonely. I realized that I was very much a single again." One day a friend wanted to see a certain movie. She suggested they go together. "'Yes,'" the friend said, 'if David does not want to see the movie, I'll go with you.' I must mention that I had known him for 50 years. Why couldn't we go together?"

Now, she does not wait for invites but asks couples and singles to her home. Yet, she's been invited to only three couple dinners. "I am not resigned to women only, but this is the way things are going. The more interesting world is for couples. I have to accept that I am a single and all that entails and make the best of it."

In retrospect, losing our husbands was the most devastating challenge of our lives. In a strange, surprising twist, it turned out to offer a gift. Eventually, we each found we were far stronger than we anticipated and able to forge new social connections on our own. Doing so became an acquired taste, and we gradually enjoyed being alone more than we anticipated. We learned more about who we are, what kind of people we liked to be with, how we liked to spend our time, and what we didn't like to do but had done because our spouse had wanted to (baseball! football! barbecues!). Most of all, being with ourselves was far better than being with someone we didn't like.

As a result of our new lifestyles and knowledge, we became more open-minded and expanded our world to include people of various ethnicities, socioeconomic groups, and sexual orientations. It's made our lives much richer and more expansive. For example, we realized that we were in the dark or not terribly well informed as we read about, met people, and had friends and acquaintances whose children and grandchildren described themselves as gay, trans, gender nonconforming, nonbinary, gender fluid, and so on. We needed a crash course in gender identity and its parlance and the difference between it and sexual orientation.

Following the Supreme Court decision to recognize same-sex marriages, a wave of them took place in states across the country. Concurrently, we began to hear of more friends and relatives proudly announcing their sexual and gender identities. This was different from what had been the norm, and we began to learn new terms of identity and sexual orientation. We embraced everyone's choices and wanted to be respectful, especially with our grown children and grandchildren.

However, we found some terms about gender to be especially confusing. We needed more clarity. Through Barbara's younger daughter, we interviewed Nick Teich, 36, PhD and LCSW, who transitioned more than 10 years ago. Teich, author of *Transgender 101: A Simple Guide to a Complex Issue,* helped us to define those terms that are most important to give people the words and meanings to make conversations around sexual and gender identity issues easier and more comfortable. From Teich we learned these terms.[3]

We're now able to look back on our marriages and share that sometimes we got in a rut with the same people and outings. It was also too much spousal or family together time when more alone and me time might have been healthier and prepared us better for our futures.

Years after becoming single, we have a different perspective on the significance of social connections than we did. As we've aged, we've witnessed more of our friends becoming suddenly single by losing a spouse or partner to death or divorce. Some chose never to marry at all or to remarry. We watched our mothers both become widows and live on their own. We've watched more TV shows like *Grace and Frankie* that detail how two women—Jane Fonda and Lily Tomlin—fared as older women losing spouses, both in this case to divorce when their husbands came out as gay. Each periodically recoupled but seemed happiest when on their own and single, each enjoying their strong friendship without male intrusion. Like them, neither of us has remarried. Our bottom line is that the importance of social connections is bigger than we anticipated when young but in a different way when older.

We've gradually learned how to connect socially with both couple and single friends. However, we suit up in our armor, so we don't feel the hurt and get wounded by the "no's" that still happen periodically. We realize that the world continues to rumble on like heavy traffic quite fine without us. Everyone is busy and torn in many directions. We've also become better at letting many know what we need since they can't read our minds, as Barbara's beau reminds her. And we try to err on the side of inclusion as Margaret's mother advised us to do. Here are a few more tips to help being included that we mastered in recent years:

- **Ask to be included.** Say, "I'm finding my Fridays and Saturdays particularly lonely and long. Might I join you some time out at dinner or take you out?" Be prepared for hesitation or an answer of "no." Some will be honest and tell you that they just can't. Try with someone else. Think of it as looking for the right job.
- **Focus on female friends who are married, attached, or single.** You might even get asked or be asked to go on a vacation together. Explain that you don't have to be attached at the hip.
- **Host a dinner or cocktail party at home.** Bring together singles and couples. If people ask what they may bring, let them help. It doesn't have to be fancy or expensive. Barbara hosted a casual dinner after a gallery opening, and it became an excuse to grill sliders and have a hodgepodge of her new village friends see her home. Margaret feted in her home symphony musicians after debut concerts with sparkling wine and hors d'oeuvres.

- **Ask two couples or a couple and some singles to be your guests at a restaurant.** Barbara's mother often did this when she became a widow; Barbara followed her example. If that's not in your budget, pick up the first round of drinks or buy a bottle of wine.
- **Organize a holiday gathering**—a trim-a-tree fete for Christmas, a latke party for one night of Hanukkah, a Seder come Passover, a Valentine's Day themed dinner, or a Halloween costume party—and get kitschy with decorations. Include a grab bag for extra fun.
- **If you want to start to date and become part of a couple, heed advice from Lisa Copeland** in Cleveland, Ohio, a leading internationally recognized love coach and dating expert for women over 50. She's the Amazon best-selling author of *The Winning Dating Formula for Women Over 50.* Here's her advice:

#1 Begin by making your own happiness a priority!

What does this have to do with dating? When you're happy, you glow. When you glow, men are attracted to you. Happiness begins inside you and is complimented by the quality men you meet. Get your inner mojo fired up by finding things to do daily that make you happy. This can be as simple as buying a new book you've wanted or taking a bubble bath and reading a book. It just has to make you happy.

#2 Create a *Single Girlfriends List.*

When my 24-year marriage ended, I wasn't ready to date. I recognized I needed some time to heal. Yet I didn't want to spend every Friday and Saturday night alone with my dog and the TV. So, I began asking friends if they knew other single women I could go to the movies or dinner with. This was one of the best things I ever did. Not only did I have fun on the weekends while I was single, but when I began dating, I had amazing support from a friend who understood what it felt like to be single and dating again. This week, think of all the single women you know.

#3 Accept yourself where you are today versus competing against an earlier version of you.

I know how hard it can be to look in the mirror and see the 50+ version of you. You start judging yourself, wondering what man is going to love a woman this age. To set the record straight . . . you're not old! Heck, 60 is the new 40! You feel old because you're comparing yourself to how you looked at 20. Men don't do this when they look at you. Their only point of reference is what you look like right now. And many men will love how you look. Attracting a good man starts with loving yourself first. So today, find 10 good things you love about you and start reminding yourself about how awesome you really are!

#4 Learn from your past mistakes.

When working with my clients, we look at all the men they've been attracted to in the past. Clients have huge Aha! moments when they see they've been unsuccessfully dating the same guy repeatedly without realizing it.

Once we've discovered the patterns, together we create what I like to call a "Red Flag List." This is a list that helps my clients see they are once again attracted to the same guy, and if they go there . . . chances are, it's going to end the same way the last one did. The reason you're attracted to the same man over and over again is because he feels comfortable to you. It doesn't mean he's good for you. Look at the men you've dated in the past and see how many of them are really the same guy with the same issues, just in different clothes.

#5 Do what it takes to make your dream of finding Mr. Right come true!

Do you remember the last time you looked for a place to live? Think about the mindset and the time you committed to interviewing real estate salespeople, checking out houses or apartments, and even looking online at Zillow so you could find the right place. Dating is like this too. It requires a full commitment to doing what it takes to find Mr. Right. You want to be working on your dating goals every day, whether it's favoring men on a dating site, flirting with men in the real world, or meeting men for coffee or a drink. Unfortunately, men don't fall out of the sky (even though it would be so much easier if they did). Since they don't, it's going to require some effort on your part to make your dream come true.

Once we each were on our own and working to improve our social lives, we learned how to connect more and be better company by practicing our roles as stars in this new type of performance. We think we have played our parts well. As one childhood acquaintance of Barbara's (who's a professional actress) said after seeing her at a party 52 years after each graduated high school, "When did you become so outgoing?" Barbara simply smiled.

Chapter Eleven

All Roads Lead (Back) Home

Margaret woke up one morning after reaching a big decision. She called Barbara to share the news that she planned to move 1,000 miles from St. Louis to New York City. She had to say it out loud to someone to make it official. The idea had been gelling for a while. The timing wasn't right until that morning when she realized that everyone in her immediate family had died or moved away. It was time.

Margaret had never discussed the idea with Barbara, who was surprised but delighted to have her writing partner and friend consider living in closer proximity. Soon after that conversation, Margaret started making plans to move, one of the most stressful challenges, along with the death of a loved one, divorce, job loss, and a major illness. What makes the difference often is being in the right headspace and doing proper planning.

People move for many reasons, some by choice and others by necessity. As a late-in-life adventurer, Margaret decided to follow her dream to move to New York City. She sought a greater sense of security by living near family as she aged. For others who move, it may be to retire to a sunny warm place that beckons and eliminates shoveling snow and risking a heart attack. Or, it may be because grown children have moved away, had children, and now want their aging parents to be closer to lessen their worries. Then, some find their homes far too large with too many steps and rooms, so they downsize to one floor, and a smaller footprint. For still others, a move may be forced upon them if they're transferred for work or because they cannot afford the mortgage or taxes. They decide to rent.

Sometimes, a house holds too many sad memories. After her divorce, Barbara kept her house longer than it made financial sense, but she wanted her grown daughters to return home to their childhood bedrooms when in college for a sense of security. Then, she no longer could justify that when they each stayed in the East after their college graduations. For others, they opt to live independently in a senior community to be around more people or they become ill and require moving to an assisted-living or extended-care/nursing facility.

There is one incontrovertible fact: at different points in our lives, we will move. As we age, we hope to do so less because of the expense, effort, time, and energy it consumes.

To understand the transition, one psychotherapist with analytical training says that how you feel about leaving the place you currently live for a new home may be greatly influenced by your attachment style. "If you're secure, it may be an adventure. If insecure with attachment issues, it can be terrifying," says Katherine M. Noordsij, LCSW, PhD in literature, certified in psychoanalysis from the William Alanson White Institute in New York City.

Noordsij explains that whether someone finds moving stressful or views it as an adventure, albeit with some trepidation, may relate to your earliest experiences with moving. "Even if the move is something that occurred recently, it can be useful to explore the associations, memories, and dreams that might reveal how location or change of location affected you as a child," she says. "What kinds of feelings might you have about having moved or never having moved? Did you stay in the same house growing up or did you move frequently? Were your parents in the military or with a company that meant you had to move often? How might those feelings influence how you feel about your present move?"

On the flipside, Noordsij suggests looking at what it might be like to start again in new surroundings. What tasks are needed to make your new place a home? She adds, "Back up and think about moving in terms of who is with you in making the move and how it will affect them, such as your kids or your partner. They, too, must make new lives for themselves. Lastly, think of images from the past such as your bedroom as a child or other rooms in your home. What feelings are associated with that? How does that affect you now as you are moving through your life and moving on?"

After her husband died, Noordsij moved from her home in Madison, New Jersey, to New York City where she had been seeing some clients. The move made sense to her.

Margaret says the same. She loves the Big Apple and knew it well from visiting her two sisters who had lived there for decades and from when her three kids had all attended college there and lived in the city at different times. More recently her older son had accepted a job there.

Still, she took her time to make the decision to move since she felt entrenched in a comfortable routine in St. Louis with good friends and a few members of her husband's family. Why go through the aggravation of selling her condo? However, as the days passed, the thought of moving to the city became intoxicating. Margaret began to picture herself there and decided she had to make the move while still healthy and energetic. Also, she no longer wanted the responsibility of owning a home, car, or even so much stuff. She could rent, live near public transportation, and walk to grocery stores, coffee shops, libraries, bookstores, concert venues, theaters, museums, and parks.

Barbara, who had moved after her divorce from St. Louis to the Hudson River Valley of New York to be closer to family, thought Margaret's idea was terrific. She gave her some unsolicited guidance, much of which is chronicled in our book, *Suddenly Single After 50*. The key nugget Barbara shared was: "If you don't like it for whatever reason, you can move back or elsewhere. Nothing has to be permanent."

CREATE A MOVING TIMELINE, THEN BUDGET, RESEARCH, AND PLAN

Noordsij gave herself a nine-month schedule. First, she would sell her home and when the house was changing hands, she would rent an apartment in New York City. Several months before she was ready to move, a friend connected her with a real estate salesperson who asked Noordsij for a wish list and price range. She started sending her listings. One day in May 2019, one of the listings was adjacent to a place where she had attended weekly meetings. "I wanted to see an apartment and went the next day," she says. "I couldn't find anything I didn't like about it after spending an hour checking it out. It had good light, a closet system, good storage, a new kitchen, and the living room was big enough for a rug I wanted to bring." As she walked from the apartment to the subway, she wondered if she should grab it. She did and that weekend it was hers. The lease started in July and she moved in August.

Margaret needed almost a year to get her ducks in order before making her move. Initially, she consulted with her financial advisors to work out a budget and see if the move was feasible. She realized that some expenses like rent, food, tips, homeowner's insurance, state taxes—New York state has the highest overall tax burden in the country—entertainment, dental work, pedicures and manicures, haircuts and coloring would be higher. However, she wouldn't have the costs of car maintenance, insurance, AAA membership, parking, personal property taxes, real estate taxes, gasoline, and big utility bills in a smaller rental space. She could also shed some magazine and newspaper subscriptions by going digital, pare cable TV to basic and one cable box and TV, take public transportation using a senior Metro card, and have a house cleaning person come fewer times a year. She came up with a Plan B in case the stock market went through a recession. Her safety net would be to rejigger her budget or move again if the city became too expensive.

She factored in several extra expenses her move would incur such as closing costs and commissions on the sale of her condo, overlapping rent, mortgage payments she might incur for a month, storage rental, and professional movers. Then, she came up with the idea of a barter—her car for the moving costs when a mover expressed interest. Other expenses emerged—packing materials; cleaning supplies; new furniture for her new hipper, smaller place; someone to help her set up her computer; new food and cleaning supplies.

She learned the wisdom of beginning the research phase after going through the financial planning one. As she began to get ready to leave, she asked herself how the place she might move to would become a home. She made a list of activities she wanted to pursue and what resources she needed—a good grocery store, bookstores, a nearby library, places to walk and hike, concert and theater venues, and lively ethnic restaurants. She investigated health care services, so important as we age, and took names of doctors and hospitals from her sisters and Barbara.

She checked out neighborhoods based on her wish list: proximity to her sisters and son on the Upper West Side. She wanted a low floor (she gets spooked living up too high) in a newish building with a doorman. Her one sister convinced her she needed a washer and dryer in her unit. To test what it might be like to live in New York City and navigate the city on her own, she rented a VRBO apartment eight months before her move and spent a week there. She also checked out potential neighborhoods of interest. Then, she was ready to move forward.

She went back to New York City and, with her two sisters in tow, hired a real estate agent and found a one-bedroom, one-bath apartment to rent in a newish building that she describes as a United Nations with a diversity of residents of all ages. The lease started August 2019, and she decided to move the beginning of September, giving her a full month before she arrived to have her sisters test all systems, clean it, stock it with certain supplies, arrange furniture, and be there when the movers arrived.

She set up a moving-day timeline like Noordsij did, which gave her some jitters that this was really happening. No turning back? Well, she could but it was becoming harder. For her this meant a simple schedule of somewhat flexible time frames, expected weather, and schedules of people helping with packing or unpacking, whether friends, family, or professionals. For example, she decided to schedule a time to put her condo on the market and then clean it once empty. Writing this all out decreased her stress and made it more real.

The process of readying the condo to sell took several months of decluttering, cleaning, and downsizing. She was moving to an apartment that was not much larger than her condo's combined dining and living rooms. She had to let go of most of the family items accumulated through the years. Curating your belongings and donating or giving away things becomes one of the toughest steps when moving. Besides the help of her sisters, some friends pitched in to organize objects and offered emotional support.

Most difficult for her and her children was parting with family collections. She went to experts to value them for sale. Most advised selling a collection as one entity rather than breaking it up, if possible. You can also sit on your computer and try to sell on your own or bring in an expert to appraise your collection and/or help sell it, which will mean sharing proceeds. Shows and events are another good way to sell a collection or through retail consignment stores. If something is valuable but there's no market for it, consider donating it to a museum, school, charity which may have a resale shop, or Goodwill, Salvation Army, or Habitat for Humanity. Know that some may not want it. Everybody else is selling things, especially brown wood furniture from the 1950s and 1960s.

When Margaret was done paring down furnishings, she hired a team of professionals to check out her home's systems to be sure nobody would try to lower her condo's price based on repairs; better for her to make the repairs in advance. She listed the condo with a salesperson she knew well, obsessively cleaned, had her salesperson hold an open house, and was delighted that the condo, priced fairly, sold within 24 hours with bids over the asking price. Margaret's salesperson held her hand and guided her through the process. Soon they celebrated.

A month before Margaret left St. Louis, she cleaned up her apartment, had her car inspected and fixed, finished some work while she still had Wi-Fi, made address changes, packed anything that wasn't perishable (letting the mover handle breakables), and figured out what she needed to pack in a suitcase to last a week. Then she stopped to take a good long look at what she was leaving behind, scheduled time to give her favorite spots in her city a good walk-through or visit, got together with various groups of friends and family to reminisce about the memories made through the decades, said final goodbyes, and encouraged everyone to visit her. She reasoned that feeling the sadness about a chapter closing were normal. Then her excitement mounted for her new life to begin.

The day she flew to New York City, it was 70 degrees with low silver-colored clouds floating across a blue sky. The maple trees were turning red, the ginkgoes brilliant yellow with leaves drifting slowly down like big flakes. Autumn in New York is perfect. Margaret remembers being delighted yet a bit scared and questioning, how and where would she fit into this bustling, chaotic place?

Moving to any new city takes work to adjust to new shopkeepers, physicians, traffic, potential new friends, and habits. New Yorkers can be far brusquer than St. Louisans but are also incredibly warm and welcoming, even strangers. Generalizations are generally terrible, Margaret learned.

How do you handle all these changes at your stage of life? So much depends on the specifics. Are you moving when the kids are in elementary school, are teenagers, you are an empty nester or retired, or are a widow or divorcee trying to make a home for yourself as a single person? It also matters what groups and activities you'll participate in, if you work, and if you can meet new people in your neighborhood. Those who live near you may be able to offer advice and help.

Even if you're an introvert, it's wise to become a joiner to find friendly faces. Look for activities that will help you get attached to your new home and begin to create positive memories, as they did for "Allison," 71, who moved from Arizona to Tennessee. She and her husband relocated to be closer to their son who had moved to the Nashville area for work. It would be a two-for-one since her daughter in Indiana now would be six hours away by car.

To check out Nashville, Allison and her husband spent a week there and looked at some properties. Nothing piqued their interest. One day a few months later, her son called and offered his mother a ticket to a major concert adding that if his parents both came to Nashville, they'd have a chance to see what it's like in another season. This time they stayed in a suburb to get a feel for life in the 'burbs and again looked at some houses.

Before they went, Allison did her research to make sure that what is important to her about their lives could be replicated in their new state. She knew it would be tough leaving her friends, but she'd make new ones, she assumed, since she's outgoing. She worked at a school and many in her area knew her. She'd miss that. The climate wasn't perfect, either, since winters are colder in Nashville. Most of the year the weather is mild. The cost of living was about the same—car insurance and registration were considerably less.

Culturally, there were concerts and fun restaurants. Since they only take beach vacations, they thought they'd be closer to the beaches. Another plus. The politics weren't perfect; however, she was sure she'd find some like-minded people. The hospitals were good, and she was confident that she could assemble a list of good doctors and dentists.

They looked at houses and found one they liked with its large lawn and oversized garage that her husband could use as a shop for his woodworking. They also perused the area for grocery and drug stores. They met some neighbors, one of whom Allison stopped to ask questions about the area. He was welcoming, provided his contact and Facebook information, and shared how to access the neighborhood Facebook page. Was she nervous about the move? "Sure, but everything fell into place. If you go in with a positive attitude, it helps."

Even before arriving, she discovered that their neighbor had cut their grass so that they followed HOA regulations. At the same time, at least 10 female and male neighbors of all ages friended her on the neighborhood FB page and shared area resources. Within days of moving in, the Southern hospitality was evident as neighbors showed up with baked goods and homemade jam. Shortly after getting settled, Allison discovered the social life there was "as little or as much as you want." She was stunned that when the holidays rolled around, they received invitations from several younger neighbors they barely knew if being with family wasn't an option.

Will they always live in their new area? "It works for us now. We're both happy to be closer to our kids. However, the house is rather big and at some point, we'd like to downsize and have less maintenance." She's not sure you can go home again but says, "I think you can if you don't expect everything to be the same. But my mind is open, and we're taking a wait-and-see attitude."

Soon after she moved, Margaret felt the change transforming and recognized strengths she didn't know she had. Within a couple of months, she was sitting in a diner pouring hot sauce on her scrambled eggs while reading the *New York Times*, traveling on subway lines, tutoring students in East Harlem, and walking along busy streets and through Central Park, where one afternoon she got caught up in a Columbus Day parade. She took a bus to the East Side to Barbara's mother's apartment for the Jewish High Holidays with Barbara's multigenerations; had glasses of wine in a posh restaurant with Barbara and a few friends whom Barbara wanted her to meet; met new potential friends for coffee many afternoons, happy hours, or dinner; and checked out different areas with her sisters, following up explorations with coffee or dinner, movies, concerts, Broadway shows, and museum visits. She was in her 70s and living the life!

As the days rolled by, Margaret made more new friends while doing volunteer projects, and rushed from her apartment to physical therapy for a sore knee where she'd be in the same exercise space as Howard Stern—yes, that Howard Stern. She attended concerts at the New York Philharmonic, courtesy of her elder son who works there, and through him met people including a famous male movie star who invited her to his home for a Sunday afternoon football game (where she met another famous female star). She was also her host's guest at Thanksgiving and

Christmas dinners. Most mornings, she was perched at her computer working like she had always done regardless of being in a new location. But here she had a glorious view of the Hudson River across to New Jersey, an unexpected perk that hadn't been on her original must-have list. There still is something familiar and comfortable about having the routine of work in the morning. She reserved her afternoons for exploring her new town.

In six weeks to six months after a move, you may find yourself "taking your temperature" to see how you're doing. Margaret did. She reevaluated and wanted to test if she needed to make changes. The first six months in New York City for Margaret were glorious. Then, the coronavirus hit, and she became confined to her small apartment. At first, she questioned why she had made the move. Would it have been different in St. Louis? Probably not, she decided, but the rent would have been less, she would have had felt freer by driving a car, and she might have found it easier to venture out to less crowded supermarkets, parks, and friends' yards with a mask. Going back might be difficult, though she temporarily pondered that as an option. However, she remembered that life there represented the past. She knew she could make the best of a bad situation, like everyone else was, and hoped "normal" life would soon return.

For Barbara, who's been in her post-divorce location for a decade, she knows it was the right move, a big unknown at the time since she didn't know her village or residents but trusted a cousin's advice. She, too, viewed it as an adventure. From her prior moves to St. Louis and Chicago, she knew to try to lay the groundwork and find resources before she arrived. After she moved in and had beds set up, she invited friends to visit her in her charming circa 1797 home, which gained an addition in the mid-1800s and became known as the Ehlers house. She often felt the equivalent of author-turned-innkeeper Bob Newhart on the eponymously named 1980s TV sitcom.

Living in a walkable community has become more important to Barbara as she ages. She lives steps from the heart of her village. Although she doesn't have friends she's as close with as those from her other "lives," she's been able to make good ones who call her up to make dates and checked on her during the COVID-19 pandemic of 2020. She also developed a daily pre-pandemic routine with work interspersed with exercise, cooking, and visiting shopkeepers and her library. She's learned more about herself. "I love that there's less of a hierarchy here with people coming from so many backgrounds, ethnicities, religions, political persuasions, and professions. We're a small village where people come to meetings and speak up about how they want to live," she says. She barely misses big-city life.

Yet, after hitting 71, she decided she might stay for a few more years but not forever as she and the house age simultaneously. The garden, originally her happy place, has become annoying as area squirrels devoured her vegetables. "I spend too much of my income on plowing, mowing, and having groundhog and bat specialists in to remove wildlife. I don't need as much space indoors, either. A condo beckons," she says.

MOVE OR STAY PUT?

Wonder whether to stay put in your house or make a move from a beloved home, condo, or apartment? Here are some pros and cons to help you evaluate.

Pros to Staying

- The size and layout are still manageable, including climbing stairs to enter or go to a second level, and you still use all the rooms.
- Family and friends visit so you use the entire house at times.
- Costs to maintain and make repairs are manageable, and you're not becoming house poor.
- You love your location and neighborhood because it's walkable (important if you can no longer drive), near a park, and close to doctors, pharmacies, and a good hospital.
- The house is still increasing in value, and real estate taxes aren't exorbitant.
- You've paid off the mortgage.
- You have a first-floor bedroom and bath for aging in place.
- You can navigate within your home with a walker and wheelchair, and it's feasible to make accommodations to age in place.
- If you move to a condo, there will be monthly HOA fees and potential assessments.
- There is a lot of inventory on the market so your home might not generate as much buzz if you sell now.

Pros to Leaving

- It's harder emotionally and financially to deal with repairs (i.e., the kitchen and bathrooms need updating).
- It's becoming more difficult to find competent, trustworthy work-people to do repairs.
- The yard and garden are becoming an albatross—costly and difficult to maintain as you age.
- You're considering a move to a condo community that will take care of outdoor maintenance.
- Expenses are escalating—taxes, repairs, appraisals.
- You have good health and the energy to move now rather than later.
- You don't want to saddle your kids with clearing out your belongings.
- There's a great place nearby that you love, which may be all remodeled and smaller, maybe new, and has amenities such as a garage that your current home does not have. It may also have social amenities like a pool and clubhouse.
- Now's a great time to sell because there's little inventory so it's a seller's market.
- Interest rates are extremely low for those buyers who want a mortgage.
- If you sell for the price you want, you will still be under the limit for capital gains taxes—$250,000 for an individual and $500,000 for a couple based on your initial price paid plus capital improvements. If you make too many improvements and can't stay to enjoy them, it might not make financial sense to do so.
- You crave less space to manage and clean.
- You debate this decision too often and it weighs on your mind. Maybe it's time to sell.

FOR THE FUTURE

Because we're often asked what made our moves easier and what our mistakes were, we share these lessons.

- Get everything in writing when you go to sell possessions. A handshake is not a contract whether it's for the sale of baseball cards, furniture, a car, or anything else.

- Don't put belongings in storage since they might remain there forever. Sell now and save the funds!
- Know that people don't necessarily mean what they say when it comes to selling a home, condo, or belongings. *"I'll be back tomorrow to buy this or that"* (they rarely show up) or *"Can I be the first person to get into your estate sale?"* (they never came even after Margaret sent multiple emails) or *"Can I get in early to see your apartment because I am sure it's exactly what I want?"* (Margaret's real estate salesperson said, "no." One person came once the apartment was officially on the market and didn't buy it.)
- Jot down lessons for future moves so you don't forget them. One from Margaret: If you sell anything on your own, get paid in cash and not by check. Margaret learned this the hard way, in case a check bounces, and they do. From Barbara: Packing boxes yourself will take longer than you anticipate and can be hard on your body; pay for help.
- If there's an unexpected change that impacts your new lifestyle in your new city, like the coronavirus, don't beat yourself up. Any decision is usually fluid and reversible. Margaret reasons she can wait out the virus, change cities again, or if she remains, renew her lease (which she did), change apartments, or move back to her former city, though not to the same condo. She can also try Los Angeles again where her daughter lives or Montreal where her younger son currently resides.
- Heed the advice of a real estate professional you trust to weigh what to do and when. Stephanie Mallios, a salesperson with Compass RE NJ, in Short Hills, New Jersey, says she's been hearing homeowners debate with themselves where they'll move as the years creep up for as long as she's been in business, which is close to 35 years. "They evaluate if they should stay put, or downsize to a smaller home, condo, apartment, or townhouse. Many end up looking around at what's available, but then do nothing because they see the walkers, canes, and raised toilets in the elder-care facilities they look at, and think to themselves, 'I don't want to be with so many old people,'" she says. "What happens," she adds, "is because they're in denial, many miss the window of making the move on their own. While they procrastinate, they may get sick or injured and need someone to help them move or make the decision for them. It may not be to a place they would choose."

When asked for her advice, Mallios says, she tells older clients to take charge when they start being bothered regularly by the size, expenses, or upkeep—or all three—required with their existing home, apartment, or condo. With her input, she helps them decide what improvements to make so the house is most sellable for the best price, and then narrow their choices where to go. "It's all much better when they're in control rather than having a decision thrust on them," she says

Moving involves taking a huge risk. Leaving your former home means bidding adieu to friends, routines, service people, favorite restaurants and shops, possessions, and perhaps a place where you grew up or lived for a long time. It takes a while to fit in, often a year or two. There were days when Barbara wondered to herself, "What have I done by coming here where I know so few?" However, we both reasoned we had made the right decisions for valid reasons and came to consider our new homes as an exciting beginning. At an older age, most of us won't have too many more of these kinds of adventures.

Chapter Twelve

Reaching the Finish Line

Lala Land, USA—Up and at 'em. Most days start at 6 a.m. in one of the first of its kind of elder-care experiments, a peer-to-peer cohousing henhouse. Everything there is shared, from cooking to working and living. The game plan was to create a new paradigm for elderly single women to coexist happily as they aged during the last chapter of their lives.

Because Barbara rises earlier than most of her new five housemates and their shared, skilled geriatric aid, she makes the coffee daily. She next defrosts and toasts the different flavors of bagels the group has shipped in monthly from Zabar's in Manhattan. She sets the table, placing at each setting either a probiotic on a napkin or a glass for liquid Metamucil.

Margaret shows up first as Barbara is usually freshening the water in the seasonal centerpiece inspired by a garden class the women took together to bring in nature, said to improve their outlook on life and health. Wearing her pink fuzzy robe, Margaret heads out to the walkway where three copies of a daily newspaper have been tossed. They subscribe to three to avoid fighting over who gets to read which section first, part of their detailed planning. In fact, the sixsome tried to think of all possible conflicts before they settled into their one-story, prefabricated green home close to their village, so it would be walkable, which most could still navigate (some with walking aids), despite their advanced years. The front entrance was made large and hallways extra wide to accommodate walkers or wheelchairs.

Their game plan also included well-appointed shared living spaces without area rugs or electrical cords dangling to trip them, no gold lamps they would consider garish, no furniture covered by plastic as one of Margaret's late husband's elderly relatives had, and separate bedrooms for each but shared bathrooms. In addition, they decided there would be no pets to stain rugs, no messes or sloppiness permitted in public spaces, and no rummaging through the refrigerator at night.

Barbara and Margaret, who were used to writing together, hatched the idea for this living arrangement after they decided against ending up in a large independent-living community and an assisted-living place or, horrors, a nursing home. They cobbled together their idea of a small version of cohousing or The Green Project Home, which was founded to offer a homier setting than the traditional nursing home. The women drew up a list of friends they imagined being able to live with until the end.

Each would offer a different skill. Barbara would do most of the cooking while still able. Besides being the newspaper fetcher, Margaret would suggest books to read, wines to quaff, old movies to watch, and which classical music and operas to listen to. Samantha, who viewed herself as the house activist, would keep everyone informed about political and women's events, as well as when they had to buy more stamps from the U.S. Post Office to help keep it afloat (it had continued to struggle).

Martha was invited in as the house architect who could decide on changes and repairs; she also was a good basic healthy cook—she cooked lots of beans for digestive reasons. Even more important, she knew how to dye her own hair, a good talent if they couldn't get out for beauty days. Roberta was picked for her legal skills and reading contracts so nobody would be bilked out of funds as scams on the elderly continued at a furious pace. Nancy was chosen because of her sense of humor and gardening skills.

To help them age in place they knew they needed a live-in geriatric aide, so Barbara, the FB maven, posted advertisements. Barbara and Margaret, also known as the great inquisitors, interviewed prospects. When it came time to pick the person, they agreed on someone kind, patient, not bossy, and able to stand up to everyone's grown children and provide skilled medical care. She also had a car to drive them to the nearby local urgent care facility or hospital.

As a group, they sat down every Sunday afternoon to discuss problems and go over any new matters such as Martha having too many family and friends over or Samantha not respecting their rule about no hook ups. She had met someone on an outing to a hardware store when she asked him, "Which nut do you think fits best with this screw?" The group pounced when she tried to sneak him into her room. "Are you crazy?" they asked. "There are more STDs (sexually transmitted diseases) transmitted when you're old than young. Get rid of him NOW!" If not, they would enforce their rule about automatic dismissal, like being kicked off those TV islands. All the men in their lives had passed on, and they agreed not to start up again, inspired by the late actress Jane Fonda's mantra of being closed for business down there. Need we say more?

At the end of their weekly group meeting, the women always left 15 minutes for each to discuss their individual aches, pains, and ailments, or to seek group advice about anything on their minds. These were the rules. No vowel sounds and grunts allowed, the word vagina would be struck from the record, lawyer Roberta the attorney reminded everyone, and they couldn't keep uttering the same old phrases as if it were for the first time. Insults were off limits as well such as, "You left your disgusting soiled Depends in the bathroom." That was to be handled in a private conversation. And nobody was permitted to interrupt more than once. To stick to the 15-minute rule, they used a timer. Ding!

Each night at bedtime, after downing their melatonin and gathering to stretch gently, do Yoga poses, and meditate, they'd go to their separate bedrooms and fall asleep, elated that their experiment in happy-older living-together worked so well. Om.

* * * * *

Few of us could imagine having to think about where to live in the late stages of our lives. Yet, at some point, it becomes an inevitability that hangs in the air like a smell that won't fade. Many of us remember watching our elderly parents and some of our older friends grapple with the where-to-go-near-the-end-of-life decisions.

We may have felt sad about what we heard and saw and even wondered: Why can't life go on as it has with everyone able to run around, travel, exercise, eat out, volunteer, work, and do whatever makes hearts sing? Why does life have to come to a halt when those who are old are less able to climb stairs, walk without aids such as canes, remember cards at bridge or tiles with Mahjong cook, entertain, hear, and see well? Then the worst part—having fewer family members and friends in our lives. Sadly, aging changes all that and leaves big voids.

Now, suddenly, we're the ones having to face the changes and make tough decisions. Most in our age cohort would probably opt to age in place for many reasons. The main one is that it's what we're used to and more palatable than alternatives. The two of us have now considered a long list, and many of the senior facilities (assisted living or long-term care) we've visited or read about don't appeal to us and most baby boomers. While the amenities often may be plentiful, the sight of many walkers and wheelchairs, the taste of what's often institutional-style food, and sometimes the stench of urine make us want to develop a potion quickly to turn back the clock. If only.

Today we worry about so much more than our parents and grandparents did if they lived to old age—climate change, tainted air and water, bacteria and new viruses that might kill us, ventilation that's not as healthy as it might be, and social distancing that's hard to maintain for a long time if another pandemic erupts and requires us to isolate again. How will we survive without seeing our loved ones, who might only be able to wave from outside our windows in scenes that mirror what happened when the coronavirus of 2020 hit? Then, there's always the question of whether we can afford the places we like best on fixed incomes. We want to ensure we can live better, happier, healthier, and longer, but will we?

So, how and where will baby boomer active agers live? We're a generation that demands changes, lived through the coronavirus, and refuses to accept the norm without research and questioning. Will we downsize? During the pandemic, many found that downsizing would not have allowed enough space to isolate. This allowed and encouraged family members to return home and shelter together.

"Aging in place is going to mean aging with more space," predicted Nora Super, senior director of the Milken Institute's Center for the Future of Aging, in an article titled "What Comes Next" by David Hochman in *AARP Bulletin*'s June 2020 issue.

Robert and Edward live in a large condo and have no plans to downsize. They both contend the condo might be large, but they love to entertain their many friends and large families. It's all on one level.

"As long as we can afford it, why not stay?" says Robert, who adds that he'd like to age in place as long as "I'm manageable with a reasonable level of convenience for Edward. If that doesn't work, we might end up moving to an upscale facility or what I call a 'dependent/independent' living place."

After the most recent viral epidemic, more architects, developers, and healthcare providers started to redevelop available end-of-life housing with better air filtration systems, more UV light systems that kill viruses, more private rooms with bathrooms, and more hand-washing and disinfectant stations. We expect an ongoing stream of new choices due to the burgeoning elder population and those who can't—or don't—opt to age in place. Some are exciting and give us hope.

COHOUSING

Our fantasy version is a smaller riff on most cohousing options. It appeals because it's a more social option than aging in place, and we get to choose our roomies and our geriatric aid. We know that people need people. Cohousing started in Europe in the 1970s to create intentional neighborhoods where people collaborate to create a strong sense of community while retaining their independence and individual homes. American architects Kathryn McCamant and Charles Durrett traveled to Denmark where it began, to study the trend, then designed the first U.S. prototype in Davis, California, which was finished in 1991. They also cowrote the book *Cohousing: A Contemporary Approach to Housing Ourselves* based on their experiences, which introduced this housing concept to the English-speaking world.

Cohousing usually consists of 12 to 40 homes—single-family, townhouse, apartment, or condo—in proximity. These communities range in location and density, including urban, suburban, and rural settings. Common facilities are integral—a building or spaces for all to share amenities such as a dining room, living room, kitchen, and gardens. Walkability is usually encouraged, with parking typically relegated to the periphery. Most are intergenerational, welcoming people of all ages, but there is also a growing interest in senior cohousing communities more focused on supporting each other as we age.

What makes these communities work is that owners have chosen this type of neighborhood. They find they benefit from the closer connections among neighbors and have direct input into how the community is managed over time, unlike some of the other current independent senior housing or end-of-life institutional housing options. The communities are democratically run with residents/owners choosing to live together and making choices on all sorts of matters from how large or small homes can be, to how to save costs with community work days, to how to support each other during crises like the COVID-19 pandemic of 2020. This may not appeal to some who crave more isolation and privacy.

Among the changes McCamant has witnessed is that the next generation—young families—is showing up, now proving that this concept continues to succeed, and there seems to be more interest in nonurban areas due to the COVID-19 pandemic of 2020 and the fact that many may not have to go in regularly to an office to work, another result of the pandemic. "You can be a techie and work from an outlying area rather than be in San Francisco [or the city center] all the time," she says.

Leslie Arden, 72, a licensed real estate broker who formerly lived in California and now lives in Queens, New York, will move from her apartment when her cohousing community, Rocky Corner, in Bethany, Connecticut, outside New Haven, is finished. After she relocated back East to be closer to her son and his family, she started missing her friends and being part of a tight-knit group. One day watching a news program on cohousing, her interest was piqued, and she began to research the possibilities in her East Coast area. Although she looked at several options, Rocky Corner appealed most for its large 300-acre farm parcel, philosophy of permaculture agriculture, and being self-sustaining. Also, the layout was interesting—30 houses arranged close to one another on five acres in duplex and triplex, energy-efficient condos of one, two, or three bedrooms. There also was a parking area on the edge of the site out of view, and a large common building for shared activities. Another plus was its proximity to the culture of New Haven and a bit farther away from the bustle of New York City (a mere 81 miles). The demographics were right for her as well, providing a mix of residents in their 60s and 70s as well as many younger residents, some with children.

Another advantage is that while the community was being built, she was able to choose materials and design features and electrical wiring for the two-bedroom unit she selected. A bonus was having time to get to know the owners and finding them to be like-minded. Also, the loosely run structure with a requirement to donate six hours a month to some volunteer activity needed to run it appealed to her. At the same time, no one is forced to participate in any activity and can socialize, share meals, trails, and public spaces if they choose to do so.

Many cohousing communities now reflect a wide range of ages, and often permit children or grandchildren if a multigenerational family wants to live near one another but not under the same roof. The cohousing model has grown in popularity—there are almost 170 suburban, rural, and urban examples in the United States and another 140 under development. A growing number of these communities are for seniors to enable older adults to live with their age cohort. More cohousing options are likely to emerge as the population ages and learns of this possibility, says McCamant, who now heads her own cohousing solutions development consultancy in Nevada City, California, where she lives in a cohousing community.

To keep the peace and set standards of what's allowed in these housing arrangements, most include in their community bylaws a method to resolve disagreements, which naturally occur, and often around such issues as whether pets are allowed, how many and what kind, if children are permitted, and how old they must be. Know these in advance of getting serious about a community.

AGING IN PLACE

Aging in place may sound terrific—and this is why so many consider the option as their years add up. The reality is that it's only great if the apartment or home is safe and set up properly to help its occupant thrive on their own. Often that requires adapting the space to accommodate a wheelchair or walker and overnight aides when health challenges worsen. As previously stated, aging cannot correct its main downside: loneliness.

Lisa Cini thinks such decisions as where older adults want to live and how should be made by both the elderly person, if cognizant, and prime family members. "Older people can get very set in their routines. They may have lived in the same home for 20 years or longer and don't want to move. This may all be well and good but typically it's not, especially in a colder climate when going outside can mean a possible fall. Additionally, it can become a burden on the family. The elderly family member may begin to mess up their medications, lose bladder or bowel control, become less able to walk, or not able to remember they started to cook something and leave it on the stove. That's when the family needs a backup plan and may have to make a change. These plans need to be personalized for each individual and family; they are not prescriptive." It may require bringing in a caregiver.

If their home is paid off, they may be eligible to take a reverse mortgage and use the loan from a bank to get a monthly payment that may help pay for the aide. Long-term care insurance can also help if it's been purchased. These financial matters should be discussed with the family's financial professional or accountant.

ACTIVITIES OF DAILY LIVING (ADL)

Before making any housing choices as we age, it's important to assess our ability to continue to execute the six routine activities of daily living (ADL) without assistance. They are eating, bathing, getting dressed, toileting (continence), mobility, and transferring (going from bed to chair and vice versa). Performing these standard functions is critical in determining whether we can live in an independent housing facility or if we need assisted living or long-term care and health coverage, including Medicaid, Medicare, or long-term care insurance.

AGE-RESTRICTED OR AGE 55-PLUS COMMUNITIES

These types of facilities go by different names but share similarities. The senior residents, typically 55 years old but often much older, still live independently, in an apartment, condo, townhouse, or house that they rent or own. Again, living independently means they must be able to perform the six activities of daily living (ADL).

Most of the communities organize daily activities such as art classes, book clubs, exercise classes, pickle ball, musical concerts on site, and bridge. Some also offer one or two meal options a day or snacks. The reason many occupants move in is to be with their peers and to shed the responsibility of home maintenance. At the same time, they are not ready to give up active living and many still drive, can take public transportation, or call in their own health-care providers for medical needs. Some of the places even have a personal care department where health-care aides are on call as needed.

Cini describes some of the newer versions of this type of community as a "mashup of a country club." Margaret's mother lived in one, and she often compared it to a cruise ship with its meals and activities. These communities can be found almost everywhere—in urban areas and suburban and rural neighborhoods. Regardless of location, they can be expensive, especially in states like New York, Connecticut, the DC area, and California, sometimes as much as $25,000 a month, though often less. So much depends on the geographic area, size of unit, amenities offered, services such as meals, and organized activities. Many are renovated every seven years, which can add to the costs but also provide a fresh look.

A relative by marriage of Barbara's moved with her boyfriend to such a community in New Jersey to be close to her two daughters and grandchildren. The couple liked one of the one-level, two-bedroom condominiums. There are also attached condo-style homes of varying stories and other condos arranged in a courtyard U-shape. She liked that the community contained 800 units with more than 1,500 residents, so there would always be enough people with whom to socialize. A club house has rooms for bridge and other card games, ping-pong and pool tables, a library, auditorium, meeting rooms, indoor and outdoor swimming pools, aerobics room, outdoor tennis courts, bocce court, and walking paths.

They have enjoyed the activities and people they've met and consider some new close friends. "We really lucked out. We're a very friendly community, and it's easy to make friends. We pride ourselves on the fact that when someone new comes, we try to incorporate them right away into activities," she says. A lifestyle director orchestrates activities of more than 350 clubs with regular announcements made to remind residents. There are a few restrictions about kids and grandkids visiting such as each owner can have only four guests at the outdoor pool on weekends.

Residents pay for their condo as they might in any community, but there are also additional monthly maintenance fees. They pay their real estate taxes separately. Barbara's relatives plan to stay put as long as they can live independently. "We are totally happy. We've met many people we like, some of whom eventually bring in help for 12 or 24 hours, which they can do here," she says. However, if health greatly declines, the occupant may need to move to a place with much more care.

There are two mistakes Barbara's relative feels she made. Their condo faces north and receives little light. She says if she had to do it again, she'd probably put this on her list of must-haves. Furthermore, they have a small balcony, which prevents her boyfriend from gardening. "Many people who move into a retirement community move from single-family homes where they may be taking these things for granted. I know that was the case with us," the relative says.

LIFE CARE OR CONTINUING CARE RETIREMENT COMMUNITY (CCRC)

This solution offers what the names suggest—care for life with a continuum of health assistance attention in the same place throughout a person's life. It may take place in the same building but in a different area or sometimes in separate buildings on the same campus.

Many are set up to "buy into" the community by signing a contract for what you receive. You or your heirs receive back a portion of that amount—often 60 to 70 percent—if you move away or die, says Mark Francis, vice president of special projects, team, and family experience for Schonberg Care, a long-term care company with 14 independent, assisted living, and memory care communities across Louisiana, Mississippi, and South Carolina. The company is based in New Orleans.

There is also a monthly fee, the equivalent of an assessment or HOA that covers maintenance and other incidentals. Extra expenses might include beauty salon appointments, massages, and purchases from a small grocery or gift shop on site. Some are also set up as rentals.

Lou and Jane moved to Peconic Landing, a CCRC on North Shore Long Island, after selling their New York City apartment. They kept a vacation home nearby in the Hamptons to be able to get away during the summer while they are mobile. They were introduced to Peconic Landing when they helped a close friend look for a retirement community with lifetime care for her final years. "As she explored apartment options, we all became impressed with the rich possibilities this place offered," says Lou, a long-time shelter magazine editor. "First, there was the range of health care options—assisted living, rehab, long-term, and memory care—a basic requirement; then, the wide choices of apartment layouts. We chose a two-bedroom, two-bath unit with generous-size living room, den, kitchen, laundry room, and balcony. Our monthly maintenance includes three meals a day, weekly housekeeping, use of a gym, indoor swimming pool, Monday night movies, musical and lecture events, discussion groups, bridge games, etc."

The unexpected bonus has been new friendships the couple developed. "We love our lazy chats after breakfast or lunch in the Bistro, and easy-to-arrange dinners for four, six, or more in the more formal dining room overlooking Long Island Sound. We still have our second home, but our first summer there we found ourselves missing our new friends and our new home at Peconic Landing," he says.

The biggest downside for some in this living arrangement may be the tendency for residents to get cliquish like high school children with little constraint. "However, the upside is the chance to have all needs met on site, including rehab for broken bones or being able to move within the community if health deteriorates," Cini says.

She advises potential residents to visit a community they're considering multiple times to talk to residents about what they like and don't like and even ask the staff if they have a guest room where they might stay overnight. "You want a diversity of people in most cases but also enough like-minded ones so you're happy," Cini says. Be sure to inquire if you come as part of a couple what happens if one member has to move to another unit for greater care or to downsize, if one dies, to a smaller unit to offset the cost of the second room or unit.

For peace of mind, many find this model advantageous since they know they will have the option of more advanced care if required rather than have to move to another facility. If serious, consider putting your name on a list since many are full and require waits to get in. Long-term care insurance may cover some or all costs if care is necessary, Francis says. Some accept Medicare or Medicaid, particularly at the nursing home stage.

NURSING HOME (LONG-TERM CARE)

While nursing homes, also called long, extended, or skilled care, may be part of a life care community, they also may operate independently. We each have seen several nursing homes. Most are not places where we are eager to end up. Barbara's late father spent six weeks in a small one in suburban New York when her mother could no longer care for him at home with an aide due to his Alzheimer's disease. He would stay up all night—what is known as "sundowning"—hide money, threaten her mother, and wander through the house. The nursing home her mother selected was clean, the aides paid attention to him, the food was decent, and the owner was kind when he died.

The same applied to the facility Margaret's mother spent her last few months living in going from independent living to extended care after falling. She had rehab at the nursing home and needed so much care at that point that she stayed. Since her mother lived on the campus, the family was aware of the standards of the facility, and it was about the best in St. Louis at the time.

The nursing home prototype we consider most palatable and cutting edge comes under the umbrella of The Green House Project. Seniors each live in their own bedroom with bathroom and share a living-dining room and kitchen in a small home setting with 10 to 12 others. There may be several of these homes on the same site.

Skilled caregivers provide round-the-clock care within each house and tend to residents' medical and food needs. Founded in 2003 by Dr. William (Bill) H. Thomas, a geriatrician, and in partnership with Steve McAlilly, CEO of Mississippi Methodist Senior Services, the men decided to develop an alternative to institutional-style nursing homes. Since its inception, the Baltimore-based nonprofit has partnered with organizations to oversee the construction of 300 homes across the country with shared similarities of the importance of daylight, private bedrooms and bathrooms, and quality care, says Susan Ryan, senior director. During the 2020 COVID-19 pandemic, the model held up well since it offered the benefit of "human connectiveness with social distancing," Ryan says.

Anyone who considers a nursing home must do their homework because of the wide variances among the options. Check medical care, cleanliness standards, ratio of caregivers to patients, extra activities, and additional or hidden fees. The federal government offers a checklist on its www.medicare.gov site with a good list of questions to pose. The checklist can be printed and used as you tour and evaluate a nursing home. Note also that the number of occupants in nursing homes is decreasing, according to the CDC. One factor may be the staggering cost; another is that more prefer to live out their days by aging in place at home.

Some questions we suggest asking while searching:

- Is the nursing home Medicare or Medicaid certified? Certified means the home passed an inspection conducted by a state government agency. Medicare only covers care from nursing homes that are certified, the site explains.
- Are the nursing home and current administrator licensed in that state?
- Does the nursing home have a bed available?
- Does it offer specialized services like a special care unit for a resident with dementia or ventilator care?
- Is the nursing home located close enough for friends and family to visit? Are there specified visiting hours, and can family members just pop in?
- Are there resident policies a visitor must follow?
- Are there extra charges for other services like a beauty shop?
- Have you checked the nursing home's star rating on Medicare.gov?
- Can residents still see their personal doctors?
- Do residents have a choice of food items at each meal?
- Can they have meals delivered to their rooms?
- How are you prepared for the next pandemic?

The checklist also suggests that anyone considering placing an elderly loved one in a nursing home or moving in themselves should ask how often there will be resident and family group meetings, which staff are in on those meetings, and if they or other family members may attend. Also, find out what the facility plans for future improvements, staffing, handling another pandemic, and other changes. Furthermore, the checklist suggests visiting a nursing home a second or third time on a different day of the week and at a different time since staff and shifts change. The key is to have a full picture of how well patients are cared for, the cleanliness, certification rules, and meals.

Also know that prices vary widely. In Barbara's Upstate New York area, the charge at one nice but no-frills nursing facility was more than $500 a day in 2020 for a private room with bathroom, the only kind it offers. The room includes a bed, dresser, private bathroom, and vinyl flooring so carpeting won't get stained or cause trips or falls. Nationwide, many cost more in large cities like New York, Boston, Chicago, and Los Angeles and less in smaller cities and more rural areas. Again, so much depends on how nice or basic the facility is, its rooms, amenities, and other services.

Medicare, Medicaid, and long-term care insurance pay many of the fees, based on policies, so know what a member's plan offers. Most facilities include a blend of patients, though the number of Medicaid patients may be more limited, says Francis. Also, if Medicare is not accepted and you pay out of pocket, find out how much is tax deductible.

CONCERN ABOUT COSTS

Financial advisor Joseph Hearn suggests two potential strategies to help pay for certain expenses. The first is to use a permanent insurance policy that you no longer want by cashing it in or, if you can get more money, a "life settlement" (information at lifesettlements.com). That way you are no longer paying the premium. Or, use the cash value in that insurance policy to buy a new paid-up life-insurance policy with a long-term care rider. This new policy will act as life insurance once you die. Where it differs is that it also will give you a multiple of the face value of the policy in long-term care benefits. This kind of policy typically has an option that allows you to terminate the policy for a full refund if you decide you don't want to buy a new paid-up life insurance policy with a long-term care rider.

When it comes to availability, Hearn says they can be found but cautions, "If you're going to pay for one by converting an existing permanent policy that you have, then of course you'd need to have an existing permanent policy. That will shrink the pool of potential people that could use this strategy. However, if you don't have an existing policy, you can just buy a life policy with a long-term care rider by paying for it out of pocket. People would just need to check with their insurance advisor for availability and advice," he says.

A second way to curtail costs is to consider a move to a state where taxes on income and other daily expenses are lower. However, it's not so simple as factoring in just one number. Most retirees have income from a variety of sources such as a pension, Social Security, work, savings, IRA distributions, and dividend income, Hearn says. "Different states tax those income sources differently," he says. Some states like Florida, Alaska, Texas, South Dakota, Nevada, Washington, and Wyoming have no personal income tax. Many exempt Social Security benefits from tax or exempt military and governmental pensions.

"Know too that there are all kinds of taxes on living costs to weigh in a new location such as real estate taxes if you buy rather than rent when you move, along with different sales taxes. Do your research and study the cities and states you might consider. Also don't forget to consider things like proximity to family and friends, climate, cost of living, quality of medical facilities, entertainment, and outdoor activities," Hearn says.

HOSPICE AND PALLIATIVE CARE

These end-of-life choices help provide short-term care for us and our loved ones. Hospice (where therapies to keep a patient alive aren't used but patients are kept comfortable and pain free) is considered one form of palliative care and is available in the last six months of life, Cini says. Sometimes someone may be a candidate, then recover so it's no longer needed, but then may be needed again, Cini adds. Though many equate palliative care with a terminal illness in the last six months or so of life, it can be used for pain management and chronic disease. In each case, a physician assesses what's best for the health challenges at hand, if a person is eligible.

THIRD-PARTY ADVOCACY

In making these end-of-life decisions, many families decide it's worth their time and money to hire a third-party expert to help navigate the increasingly complex legal and medical options. Teri Dreher, a registered nurse and board-certified patient advocate, founded two companies that wade through the senior care morass. They are a resource center for the range of options. Her companies in the Chicagoland area, North Shore Patient Advocates, www.northshorern.com, and Seniors Alone Guardianship and Advocacy Services, www.seniorsalone.org, have a staff of skilled healthcare experts that handle a wide range of needs, from hiring someone to take an elderly person to the doctor and dental appointments on a regular or special needs basis to finding someone to move in and take care of a person on a full-time basis.

They might also find someone to help pay bills and understand different medical charges or decide which senior living option might work best for a client's needs and budget. "They may prefer a CCRC or be ready for a nursing home. If they have long-term care insurance, they may be able to afford more than if they didn't," Dreher says. At the same time, she says, "Some of the newer policies severely limit what they provide."

Their service works like this. Before her staff helps families make decisions, someone will meet with the elderly person and/or their family members to conduct an in-depth assessment of needs. Perhaps, for example, they want to know if their home is safe enough to age in place or if they are mentally competent enough still to live alone safely. Generally, the assessment runs about 90 minutes for $400, depending on the individual situation.

For those who live in other areas of the country, Dreher recommends finding a "professional care manager" or "patient advocate" by googling those types of job descriptions or going online to The Aging Lifecare Association, www.aginglifecare.org, which has a huge database of social workers and nurses who perform community care management, according to zip code location. Two other good organizations to tap into are The Alliance of Professional Health Advocates, www.alphadvocates.org, or the National Association of Healthcare Advocacy, www.nahac.com.

Dreher adds, "Ask anyone you or family members are considering hiring detailed questions: How long have you been in business? What's your educational background? What special skills do you offer in helping me or a family member? How much do you charge per hour? How much do most aides get per hour? Would you provide at least two referrals I may contact? Then, trust your gut with all your information in hand. If for any reason you don't find the person a good fit, be prepared to switch."

USING TECHNOLOGY
TO HELP US LIVE INDEPENDENTLY

Regardless of our housing choice as we age, technology can change how we live by helping us remain more independent, Cini says. Many of our aging parents never used technology tools and, if alive, still don't feel able to start now. We've had challenges with some newer ones, too, so we get that technology is not always our friend. When Barbara and her daughters sent photos or wanted to FaceTime with their 100-plus-year-old mother/grandmother, it was not something she could do. So, the family sent photos of the youngest generation to her Mom's aide on their iPhones, so she could see her great grandsons from afar.

Our generation of baby boomers will be able to use much of the smart technology in our homes in our elder years. We already have embarked on this adventure. According to an updated poll by the Pew Research Center, some 59 percent of adults over the age of 65 are digitally connected and familiar with Skype, FaceTime, Zoom, Loop, WhatsApp, and WeChat.[1] Some of us used Zoom so much during the 2020 COVID-19 pandemic that we experienced fatigue with it.

It seems that monthly, more new high-tech tools—apps, gadgets, and services—emerge. Cini lists many on her website, www.bestlivingtech. com.

Laurie M. Orlov, certified in geriatric management, founded Aging and Health Technology Watch, based in Port St. Lucie, Florida, www. ageinplacetech.com, to conduct market research to review tech products on her website. Her goal is to help those who are 65 and older age at home. The first step, Orlov told us, is to have high-speed Internet in place since so many products are dependent on that to work well. "With the right tools, you can order food online, have goods and services delivered, listen to music, have a health consultation with a doctor, read a book, find out the weather, and so much more," she says. Some tools can also keep you company such as robotic pets for those not able to get out and enjoy a walk.

Prices vary widely but having them may defer some costs associated with hiring outside caregivers to get up and answer a doorbell or monitor blood pressure. Various lines of virtual reality devices for entertainment have flooded the market. Put on the headset and you can go on a virtual tour of cities you've visited in the past or would love to see.

In the future, Cini would like to see technology that combines proper orthotics, dentures, eyewear, hearing aids, and exoskeletons. "If we can up our game on our senses, being able to see and hear properly, having our teeth fit and not be worried about them falling out, and have the proper orthotics and shoes or exoskeletons to reduce falls or drop foot that would be incredible," she says.

NAVIGATING CHOICES

As we begin to weigh choices for where and how to live in our elder years, we compare locations, quality of care provided, amenities, and budgets. While aging in place may seem the best solution, we know that it can be physically challenging and socially isolating. Too often in that situation, our age group may fall when they can't see in the dark, leave food on the stove cooking that can start a fire, forget to take medications or brush teeth, and become sad and depressed when alone too much. Cutting-edge voice-activated devices using artificial intelligence and virtual reality tools that do not require anyone to leave their beds or couches may help keep everyone healthy, entertained, and minimize certain risks to remain safely and comfortably at home. Yet, they don't compensate for in-person contact with a loved one.

At some stage, a grown child or paid aide may need to get involved, yet both may get sick and be undependable. That's why we believe a communal setting might be better for physical and mental well-being.

The goal that the two of us now strive for is to savor each day of our lives. We try not to look too far ahead, except to be aware of the options if we need to move and decide what's best based on location, medical treatment, friendship, family, finances, and hobbies—so we won't overburden family or ourselves. Finding that place is our next big challenge.

Epilogue

Is Our Inner Cake Baked?

How We Evolve as We Age to Live in the Moment

Many of us live under the illusion that our personalities are set once we become adults. We've all heard someone say a variation of: "Wow, whatever is in her head comes out of her mouth. She never changes."

So many of us seem to maintain the same spiritual beliefs for years, or never change political parties, keep the same tight circle of friends, eat the same foods and sometimes same meals, travel to the same places (when we used to travel), and have the same annoying habits.

Are our inner cakes always baked so well that we won't tinker with the recipe for what's most important—who we are, what we do, and how we do it? We used to think so. It was easier to do the same things in part to maintain a semblance of stability since, as we learned with age, nothing stays the same, and certainly not the world around us.

When we really thought about ourselves and what's been important over time, we realized our personalities have undergone big transformations as we adapted to new people in our lives through births, marriages, new locations, homes, jobs, financial situations, health challenges, disappointments, and successes. We just hadn't always been keenly aware of the shift in our thinking and behavior.

Sometimes we had to change when circumstances were thrust upon us, as in the case of each of us losing our spouses. They had helped to shape so much of our lives over the prior decades. It took work, but we crafted new lives as singles. In our late 60s—and particularly after our 70th birthdays—other changes happened, sometimes much slower, which affected us physically, emotionally, and mentally. The bottom

185

line in each case was the same. We needed to adjust our behavior to cope. This time we knew better how to take charge and evolve as we accepted the fact that the human species is far from fully baked as it moves along the continuum of the life cycle. Experts confirm this to be true, if we are to be happy, safer, and fit better into the world around us.

In his popular book *Successful Aging: A Neuroscientist Explores the Power and Potential of Our Lives*, author Daniel J. Levitin cites Louis R. Goldberg, considered the father of modern-day scientific conceptions of personality. Goldberg has found personalities can change. Based on Goldberg's findings, Levitin says, "You can improve yourself at any stage of life, becoming more conscientious, agreeable, humble—any number of things. We tend to think of personality traits as being durable, enduring forever. (Think of the curmudgeon, Larry David, in TV's *Curb Your Enthusiasm*.) But personality traits are malleable. And the degree to which habitual traits drive our behavior, is influenced by the situations we find ourselves in and by our own striving to improve ourselves, to become better people."[1]

Margaret remembers her Mom mellowing with age and becoming less volatile in her interactions with friends and family. Barbara found her mother lost her filter more often after 90, voicing thoughts she would have been appalled at expressing when younger. "Oh, that's not really her," some said, excusing her behavior. However, Barbara sometimes wondered if it really was her, just an older, more authentic version.

In interviews for this book, many women confirmed that they, too, had evolved and continue to do so. They told us that over time they have become more adventuresome, stubborn, biased, political, funnier, sexier, generous, narcissistic, compassionate, flexible, patient, and kinder. Sometimes the changes were brought on by big losses and huge events such as 9/11, the 2008–2009 economic collapse, or the COVID-19 pandemic of 2020, and other times because they were tired of thinking and doing things the same way. The change most shocking to us came from a woman whose husband died two years ago. She confessed on a Zoom call that she had evolved into a more sexual person now that she's alone. Her fantasy, she said, would be to move to the Moonlite BunnyRanch, a legal licensed brothel in Mound House, Nevada, and have as many erotic experiences as possible.

She explained, "I really miss sex and the feeling of being desired." Now that's a big shift for a small-town Midwestern gal in her late 60s, or maybe it's the inner fantasy of many women, just not shared. Perhaps there are other fantasies, unrelated to sex, that other women act on as they age.

Although our changes are a bit more run of the mill, they're significant to us. Barbara thinks she became a better parent to her grown daughters, more independent, a better friend since friendships became more important as she aged, a better listener, and more grateful. She gave up some regrets that she now considers silly—never owning a convertible, having a swimming pool, or finishing her master's degree in business administration.

Margaret has taught herself ways to slow down, which have led to fewer mistakes and accidents, curbed her tendency to offer advice when not requested, let go of expectations, shriek less when upset, and be more compassionate than when she was younger. Now on her own and with time to be more introspective, she's learned to value herself more. Her move to New York City and paying an expensive rent is something "the old Margaret" never would have done.

Unless forced upon us, change requires us to be emotionally ready. It took Margaret eight years on her own to decide to relocate 1,000 miles away. In a Zoom call during the 2020 COVID-19 pandemic, Barbara asked a handful of childhood friends if they planned to downsize in the near future. Almost all echoed the same response: "We're way too young! We're only 71 (or 70)." Only one had already made the change. Yet, the loss of a spouse or partner, financial reversals, major change in health, and the need for wider hallways, no stairs, or full-time help could quickly necessitate a new home. If we're wise at this stage, as we like to think we are, we leave ourselves open to all sorts of possibilities and toss aside old assumptions of how matters should be handled. It's never too early to evolve!

Hand in hand we might ask a much bigger questions as our clocks run down: What's the real purpose of life? This question makes us turn to our spirituality. However, what is spirituality and how does it evolve? We believe a spiritual evolution takes many forms. For some, spiritualism is synonymous with religion, rituals, and tradition. For others, it's awareness of living in the present and stepping away from distractions through meditation or reflection, then returning to focus on what gives life its greatest meaning and pleasure, including strong connections. For still others, it's a way to make the world a better place in whatever time we have.

Our spiritual evolution is a currency that the two of us have in abundance, even though neither of us considers ourselves religious. We asked several women about their spiritual evolutions. Because it was during the coronavirus pandemic of 2020, some were in a difficult place or experiencing what former First Lady Michelle Obama calls "a low-grade depression." Some confessed that life had thrown them so many curves that their spirituality was waning, but the majority said their spirituality has ramped up in their later years, particularly as they face their mortality. One woman said she had been spiritual her entire life but didn't equate it with religion. For her it was about the world around her, which inspired her paintings and designs. "Spirituality also means treating others the way you'd like to be treated. It's a big world, and it's not all about us," she says.

What we find so reassuring about evolving is that it represents endless possibilities. One dictionary definition says evolving is a slow development that takes its time to reach its final destination. We like to think of it differently—that what we leave behind will cause memories of us to continue to evolve in the hearts and minds of our children, grandchildren, and friends. And that gives us hope about the importance of pushing ourselves to step forward rather than remain stuck.

Join us in this final journey. Yes, change can be scary, but it's also incredibly freeing. The window is still open on our lives as we remind ourselves: We're Not Dead Yet.

Notes

CHAPTER TWO

1. Hugh Delehanty, "People Are Terrified of Change. Period," *AARP Bulletin/Real Possibilities*, March 2020.

2. Heidi Herman, *On with the Butter! Spread More Living onto Everyday Life* (Sioux Falls, SD: Hekla Publishing, 2020).

3. Phillippa Lally et al., "How are Habits Formed: Modeling Habit Formation in the Real World," *European Journal of Science Psychology*, Volume 40 (2010): 998–1009.

4. Suze Orman, "Your 2020 Smart Money Action Plan," *AARP Bulletin/Real Possibilities*, March 2020.

5. Bethany McLean, "How International Fraud Rings Operate and Target Older Americans," *AARP Bulletin*, April 2020.

CHAPTER THREE

1. Aminatou Sow and Ann Friedman, *Big Friendship: How We Keep Each Other Close* (New York: Simon & Schuster, 2020).

2. Lydia Denworth, *Friendship: The Evolution, Biology, and Extraordinary Power of Life's Fundamental Bond* (New York: W. W. Norton & Company, 2020).

3. Denworth, *Friendship.*

4. Natalie Angier, "You Share Everything with Your Bestie. Even Brain Waves," *New York Times,* April 16, 2018.

5. Sow and Friedman, *Big Friendship.*

CHAPTER FOUR

1. Michael Rosenfeld, Reuben Thomas, and Sonia Hausen, "Disintermediating your Friend: How Online Dating in the United States Displaces Other Ways of Meeting," in *The Proceedings of the National Academy of Sciences,* volume 116, issue 36 (2019).
2. Justin R. Garcia, Singles in America Study, Kinsey Institute, http://www.singlesinamerica.com.
3. Elizabeth Arias, PhD, and Jiaquan Xu, MD, *National Vital Statistics Report*, Centers for Disease Control and Prevention, volume 68, number 7 (June 24, 2019).

CHAPTER FIVE

1. "The Return of the Multi-Generational Family Household," Pew Research Center, March 18, 2010, https://www.pewsocialtrends.org/2010/03/18/the-return-of-the-multi-generational-family-household/.
2. "The Return of the Multi-Generational Family Household," Pew Research Center, March 18, 2010, https://www.pewsocialtrends.org/2010/03/18/the-return-of-the-multi-generational-family-household/.
3. Susan Reinhard, Lynn Friss Feinberg, Ari Houser, Rita Choula, and Molly Evans, "Valuing the Invaluable 2019 Update: Charting a Path Forward," AARP Public Policy Institute (November 14, 2019): https://www.aarp.org/ppi/info-2015/valuing-the-invaluable-2015-update.html.
4. AARP, National Alliance for Caregiving, "Caregiving in the United States 2020," AARP Public Policy Institute (May 14, 2020), https://www.aarp.org/ppi/info-2020/caregiving-in-the-united-states.html.

CHAPTER SIX

1. Anna Goldfarb, "Kick Dismissive Positivity to the Curb," *New York Times,* December 28, 2019.

CHAPTER SEVEN

1. Linda K. Stroh and Karen K. Brees, *Getting Real about Getting Older: Conversations about Aging Better* (New York: Sourcebooks, 2018).

2. "The Financial Journey of Modern Parenting: Joy, Complexity and Sacrifice," Merrill Lynch and Age Wave, https://agewave.com/what-we-do/landmark-research-and-consulting/research-studies/the-financial-journey-of-modern-parenting-joy-complexity-and-sacrifice/.

3. Suze Orman. "Your 2020 Smart Money Action Plan," *AARP Bulletin/ Real Possibilities*, April 2020.

CHAPTER EIGHT

1. "Number of People Aged 100 and Over (Centenarians) in the United States from 2016 to 2060," Statista.com, March 6, 2020, https://www.statista.com/statistics/996619/number-centenarians-us/#:~:text=This%20statistic%20shows%20the%20number,centenarians%20in%20the%20United%20States.

2. Katie Nicholl, "A Royal Spark," *Vanity Fair*, May 2020.

3. Paula Span, "When Retirement Comes Too Early," *New York Times*, August 28, 2020.

CHAPTER NINE

1. Kim Severson, "An Alabama Chef and Her Beloved Desserts Hit the Big Time," *New York Times,* May 29, 2018.

CHAPTER TEN

2. Denworth, *Friendship.*

3. Nick Teich, "Glossary of Terms," Human Rights Campaign, https://www.hrc.org/resources/glossary-of-terms?utm_source=GS&utm_medium=AD&utm_campaign=BPI-HRC-Grant&utm_content=454854043842&utm_term=list%20of%20lgbt%20terms&gclid=Cj0KCQiAvvKBBhCXARIsACTePW8VZnKW3mSSrv7aKmt0L849_1zBMpni7Csx0HA3YJ9RtUMOCQ2rNCgaAukDEALw_wcB.

CHAPTER TWELVE

1. Monica Anderson and Andrew Perrin, "Tech Adoption Climbs among Older Adults," Pew Research Center, May 17, 2017, https://www.pewresearch.org/internet/2017/05/17/tech-adoption-climbs-among-older-adults/.

EPILOGUE

1. Daniel J. Levitin, *Successful Aging: A Neuroscientist Explores the Power and Potential of our Lives* (New York: Dutton/Penguin Random House, 2020).

Bibliography

AARP, National Alliance for Caregiving. "Caregiving in the United States 2020." AARP Public Policy Institute, May 14, 2020.

Abbit, Laura. *The Conscious Caregiver.* Avon, MA: Adams Media, 2017.

Anderson, Monica, and Andrew Perrin. "Tech Adoption Climbs Among Older Adults," Pew Research Center, May 17, 2017, https://www.pewre search.org/internet/2017/05/17/tech-adoption-climbs-among-older-adults/.

Angier, Natalie. "You Share Everything with Your Bestie. Even Brain Waves." *New York Times,* April 16, 2018.

Arias, Elizabeth, and Jiaquan Xu. *National Vital Statistics Report.* Centers for Disease Control and Prevention, Volume 68, Number 7, June 24, 2019.

Ballinger, Barbara, and Margaret Crane. *Suddenly Single after 50: The Girl-friends' Guide to Navigating Loss, Restoring Hope, and Rebuilding Your Life.* Lanham, MD: Rowman & Littlefield, 2016.

Cini, Lisa M. *BOOM: The Baby Boomers Guide to Leveraging Technology, so That You Can Preserve Your Independent Lifestyle & Thrive.* Columbus, OH: (self-published), 2019.

———. *Hive: The Simple Guide to Multigenerational Living.* Bloomington, IN: iUniverse, 2017.

———. *The Future is Here . . . Senior Living Reimagined.* Bloomington, IN: iUniverse, 2016.

Clear, James. *Atomic Habits.* New York: Penguin Random House, 2018.

Copeland, Lisa. *The Winning Dating Formula for Women Over 50.* Cleveland: CreateSpace Independent Publishing Platform, 2013.

Delehanty, Hugh. "People Are Terrified of Change. Period." *AARP Bulletin/ Real Possibilities*, March 2020.

DeMure, Jeffrey. *Livable Design.* Granite Bay, CA: Fountainhead Publishing, 2018.

Denworth, Lydia. *Friendship: The Evolution, Biology, and Extraordinary Power of Life's Fundamental Bond.* New York: W. W. Norton & Company, 2020.

Druck, Kenneth. *Raising an Aging Parent: Guidelines for Families in the Second Half of Life.* London: Redwood Publishing, 2019.

Duffy, Karen. *Backbone: An Inspirational Manual for Coping with Chronic Pain.* New York: Arcade, 2017.

Dychtwald, Ken, and Robert Morison. *What Retirees Want: A Holistic View of Life's Third Age.* New York: Wiley, 2020.

Ephron, Nora. *I Feel Bad about My Neck and Other Thoughts on Being a Woman.* New York: Vintage, 2008.

Garcia, Justin R. Singles in America Study. Kinsey Institute, http://www.singlesinamerica.com.

Gawande, Atul. *The Checklist Manifesto; How to Get Things Right.* London: Picador, 2011.

Goldfarb, Anna. "Kick Dismissive Positivity to the Curb." *New York Times,* December 28, 2019.

Good, Honey. *Stories of My Grandchild.* New York: Abrams Noterie, 2019.

Goyer, Amy. *Juggling Life, Work, and Caregiving.* Chicago: The American Bar Association, 2015.

Hannon, Kerry. "Rethinking Retirement." *New York Times*, October 15, 2020.

Hearn, Joseph R., and Niel D. Nielsen. *If Something Happens to Me.* Omaha, NE: Provisio Publishing, 2004.

Herman, Heidi. *On with the Butter! Spread More Living onto Everyday Life.* Sioux Falls, SD: Hekla Publishing, 2020.

Hochman, David, "What Comes Next." *AARP Bulletin,* June 2020.

Kerr, Jolie. "A (Short) Guide to Better Boundaries." *The New York Times,* October 20, 2019.

Lally, Phillippa, Cornelia Van Jaarsveld, Henry W. W. Potts, and Jane Wardle. "How Are Habits Formed: Modelling Habit Formation in the Real World." *European Journal of Social Psychology.* Volume 40, Issue 6, October 2010, Wiley Online Library.

Lambert, Amanda, and Leslie Eckford, *Aging with Care: Your Guide to Hiring and Managing Caregivers at Home.* Lanham, MD: Rowman & Littlefield, 2017.

Levitin, Daniel J., *Successful Aging: A Neuroscientist Explores the Power and Potential of Our Lives.* New York: Dutton/Penguin Random House, 2020.

Maxwell, Nancy Kalikow. "Dating at 62: A Cautionary Tale." *The Forward,* July 10, 2015.

McCamant, Kathryn, Charles Durrett, and Ellen Hertzman. *Cohousing: A Contemporary Approach to Housing Ourselves.* Berkeley, CA: Ten Speed Press, 1994.

McLean, Bethany. "How International Fraud Rings Operate and Target Older Americans." *AARP Bulletin,* April 2020.

Munn, Chip. *The Retirement Remix: A Modern Solution to an Old School Problem.* Florence, SC: Signature Wealth Strategies (self-published), 2020.

Nemzoff, Ruth. *Don't Bite Your Tongue: How to Foster Rewarding Relationships with Your Adult Children.* New York: St. Martin's Press, 2008.

———. *Don't Roll Your Eyes: Making In-Laws into Family.* New York: St. Martin's Press, 2012.

Orman, Suze. "March AARP Bulletin: Smart Money Action Plan." *AARP Bulletin,* February 27, 2020.

Pinker, Susan. *The Village Effect.* Toronto, Canada: Vintage Random House Canada, 2015.

Polk, Betsy, and Maggie Ellis Chotas. *Power through Partnership: How Women Lead Better Together.* Oakland, CA: Berrett-Koehler Publishers, 2014.

Reinhard, Susan, Lynn Friss Feinberg, Ari Houser, Rita Choula, and Molly Evans. "Valuing the Invaluable 2019 Update: Charting a Path Forward." AARP Public Policy Institute, November 14, 2019.

"The Return of the Multi-Generational Family Household." Pew Research Center, March 18, 2010.

Rosenfeld, Michael, Reuben Thomas, and Sonia Hausen. "Disintermediating your Friend: How Online Dating in the United States Displaces Other Ways of Meeting," *The Proceedings of the National Academy of Sciences.* Volume 116, Issue 36, 2019.

Rossetti, Rosemarie. *Take Back Your Life: Regaining Your Footing after Life Throws You a Curve.* Columbus, OH: Fortuna Press, 2003.

———. *Universal Design Toolkit: Time Saving Ideas, Resources, Solutions, and Guidance for Making Homes Accessible.* Columbus, OH: Rossetti Enterprises Inc., 2017.

Rubin, Judy. Lifelessonsat50plus.com. "Long-Term Care Health Insurance: The Pros & Cons." May 17, 2019.

Schindler, Judi. *Husbands: An Owner's Manual, How to Survive a 50-Year Marriage.* Chicago: St. Michael's Publishing, 2017.

Severson, Kim. "An Alabama Chef and Her Beloved Desserts Hit the Big Time." *New York Times,* May 29, 2018.

Sher, Margery Levsen. *Child-Care Options: A Corporate Initiative for the 21st Century.* Westport, CT: Greenwood Press, 1994.

———. *Indomitables! Immigrants' Stories of Perseverance and Resilience.* Washington, DC: (self-published), 2020.

———. *The Noticer's Guide to Living and Laughing.* Washington, DC: (self-published), 2014.

Sow, Aminatou, and Ann Friedman. *Big Friendship: How We Keep Each Other Close.* New York: Simon & Schuster, 2020.

Span, Paula. "When Retirement Comes Too Early," *New York Times,* August 28, 2020.

Stroh, Linda K., and Karen K. Brees. *Getting Real about Getting Older: Conversations about Aging Better.* New York: Sourcebooks, 2018.

Teich, Nicholas M. *Transgender 101: A Simple Guide to a Complex Issue.* New York: Columbia University Press, 2012.

Zachmann, Patrick, photographer. "A New Age: Living in Our History." A Survivor's Story, Gerda Weissmann Klein. *AARP Magazine,* June/July 2019.

Index

About the Authors

Barbara Ballinger (Hudson River Valley, New York) is an award-winning freelance journalist, author, and reporter who has interviewed a variety of celebrities and experts from Tipper Gore to Martha Stewart, Danny Meyer, Rosalynn Carter, Lorraine Bracco, Doris Kearns Goodwin, and Ruth Reichl. She has covered diverse topics from business to design, real estate, entertaining, food, law, and personal finance. Her work has appeared in publications such as the *Chicago Tribune, New York Times, Crain's Chicago Business, HGTV, American Bar Association Journal, House Beautiful, Multifamily Executive, Developer, Realtor, Robb Report, St. Louis Post-Dispatch, Travel & Leisure, Triple AAA magazine, Midwest Living, Units,* and more. Of the 19 books she has authored, 10 have been with Margaret Crane. The first was *Corporate Bloodlines: The Future of the Family Firm,* and the most recent were *Suddenly Single after 50* and *The Kitchen Bible.* She and Crane blog weekly at www.lifelessonsat50plus.com. Barbara has appeared on TV and radio, including a segment about remodeling disasters on *The Oprah Winfrey Show,* about the rise in multifamily living on *Multifamily Matters,* and with Crane on NPR about their last book. She formerly worked on staff at "House & Garden Guides," part of Conde Nast, the *St. Louis Post-Dispatch* newspaper, and the National Association of Realtors magazine. She earned a BA in art history from Barnard College, Columbia University, an MA in art from Hunter College, City University of New York, and started work on her MBA.

Margaret Crane (New York, New York) is a nationally known freelance writer focusing on business, food, wine, fashion, home furnishings, and real estate. She has interviewed such luminaries as Jack Buck, Virginia Johnson, Sally Quinn, Moshe Dayan, Shimon Peres, Dr. Benjamin Spock, David Ben Gurion, Tippi Hedren, and many others. Her work has appeared in a wide variety of publications, including *Beverage Journals, Crain's Chicago Business, Family Business Magazine, Inc. Magazine, Midwest Living, The New York Times, Newsweek, Realtor, St. Louis Business Journal, St. Louis Post-Dispatch, St. Louis Magazine, St. Louis Town & Style, The Wine Spectator*, and *Your Company*. A proven author with 10 titles to her credit, Margaret's latest books with Barbara are *Suddenly Single After 50* and *The Kitchen Bible*. She formerly worked as a senior writer and researcher at a religious nonprofit, where she helped launch and maintain an award-winning website. Crane blogs weekly with Ballinger at www.lifelessonsat50 plus.com. She has also appeared on TV and radio and with Ballinger, and has spoken around the country on becoming single, including on NPR and at Barnard College. She also writes website content and does editing for nonprofit organizations and for for-profit companies. In addition, Crane tutors public school children and works with kids in foster care in New York City. She holds a bachelor's degree in journalism from the University of Missouri and started work on her master's degree in education to teach journalism, which she now uses in her work with children.

CPSIA information can be obtained
at www.ICGtesting.com
Printed in the USA
LVHW091606210821
695819LV00001B/92